WILDERNESS WANDERERS

THE 1776 EXPEDITION OF DOMÍNGUEZ & ESCALANTE

BY KEN REYHER

WESTERN REFLECTIONS PUBLISHING COMPANY®

Montrose, Colorado

ISBN 1-890437-91-3

Library of Congress Control Number: 2003108357

Cover and text design by Laurie Goralka Design

First Edition
Printed in the United States of America

Western Reflections Publishing Company®
219 Main Street
Montrose, CO 81401
www.westernreflectionspub.com

⚔ CONTENTS ⚔

Introduction

In late July, 1776, two Franciscan priests, a handful of Spaniards, Mixed Bloods and Indians left Santa Fe, New Mexico. They hoped to find an overland route to the struggling Spanish colony on Monterey Bay, on the California coast. No one knew how far Monterey was from Santa Fe but the assumption was that it could be reached before winter closed the California mountain passes. For that reason the expedition did not take any cold weather gear or clothing. It carried only enough rations for ninety days, and was supplied with several packs of trade goods to be used as good-will gifts or for barter with native people met along the way.

The expedition leaders were aware that southern California could be reached by traveling across Arizona. They also knew that this was an extremely dangerous way to go, often waterless, lacking forage for livestock, bisected by an almost impassable canyon, and inhabited by hostile native peoples. For these reasons they chose to look for a trail further north. What these explorers did not know was that terrain and other circumstances would ultimately take them much further north than they originally intended. In western Utah they ran out of food and were abandoned by their guide. The first snow of winter had already fallen. The group was badly divided as to whether to continue west or attempt to return to Santa Fe. They put the decision in the hands of God and cast lots.

For the next two months they fought their way homeward, first across the western deserts of northern Arizona, then across the gorges of the Grand Canyon, and into the dry, winter deserts of eastern Arizona. They experienced both treachery and compassion among the native peoples met along the way. Finding water for themselves and their stock had proved a daunting and sometimes impossible task, even for desert-wise travelers. They were eventually forced to subsist on their own emaciated and starving horses for meat — and there was the never-ending cold and wind. This is the story of that expedition told from the pages of the detailed journal they faithfully kept throughout the entire journey.

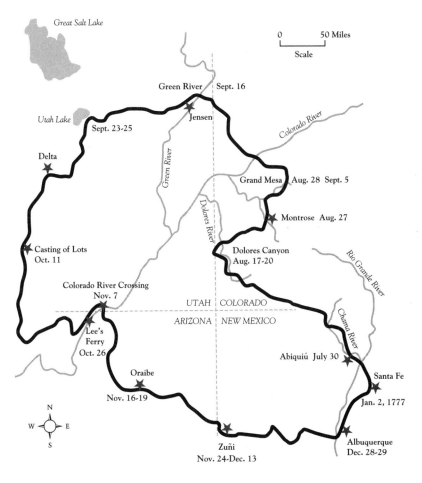

Great Salt Lake

0   50 Miles

Scale

Green River   Sept. 16

Jensen

Utah Lake

Sept. 23-25

Colorado River

Green River

Delta

Grand Mesa   Aug. 28   Sept. 5

Dolores River

Montrose   Aug. 27

Rio Grande River

Casting of Lots
Oct. 11

Dolores Canyon
Aug. 17-20

Colorado River Crossing
Nov. 7

Chama River

UTAH | COLORADO

ARIZONA | NEW MEXICO

Lee's
Ferry
Oct. 26

Abiquiú   July 30

Oraibe

Santa Fe

Nov. 16-19

Jan. 2, 1777

N
W   E
S

Zuñi
Nov. 24-Dec. 13

Albuquerque
Dec. 28-29

Domínguez-Escalante Route of 1776-77

Chapter 1

NORTH TO
⊱ SANTA FE ⊰

A handful of dust-covered riders topped a ridge and momentarily paused. Less than a half mile to the northeast they could see the languid waters of the Rio Grande River as it reflected the late afternoon sun. On the near bank they could see a scattered collection of mud brick buildings imprisoned in the dry desert earth. Each structure seemed independent of the other. There was no order — nothing to suggest plan or design. It was almost as if someone had carelessly tossed a handful of dice beside the river and had never bothered to pick them up. Father Francisco Atanasio Domínguez shifted in his saddle, his left hand shielding his eyes against the glare from the river. The priest, used to the relative opulence of Mexico City grimaced. He was not impressed with El Paso.

Domínguez and his companions, including two fellow priests, had ridden north more than 1,600 miles from Mexico City on a trail almost 200 years old. While the region in and around Mexico City had grown steadily. Little had changed in the northern frontier outposts. It was true that a few towns such as Chihuahua, a two week's ride to the south, had prospered but, for the most part, the northern colonies had remained almost stagnant. That was one of the reasons that Domínguez had come north — to make a determination why, after 177 years, the New Mexico missions still depended upon support from both the government and the church. In addition, he had also been instructed to lead an expedition west from Santa Fe and attempt to open a trail to the struggling colony of Monterey on the coast of California.

Father Domínguez had been born in Mexico City in 1740 and had joined the Franciscan Order seventeen years later. His superiors found him to be both intelligent and capable. By the time he was thirty-two his abilities, particularly as an administrator, had taken him into positions normally reserved for much older priests. His youth gave him the added advantage of being able to spend weeks in the saddle traveling from region to region, something many of his older counterparts were unwilling or unable to do. In the eyes of his superiors, he was the right man to send north.

He had arrived at El Paso September 4, 1775. In addition to the scattering of adobe buildings that the riders saw that afternoon, there were quarters for government administrators and military personnel as well as a mission station. The latter served as headquarters for the priests who served the four Indian pueblos scattered for some twenty-five miles up the river. The trail further north of the pueblos had been the subject of repeated attacks that summer and autumn by invading Comanches and Apaches. For this reason Domínguez and his two companions would be forced to spend the winter in the town. It would have been foolish, perhaps even suicidal to continue on. Domínguez, in a detailed letter to his superiors in Mexico City, explained the delay and waited impatiently for spring.

Winter passed and no word came concerning further raids. The Comanche had retreated northward to their summer hunting grounds east of the Rocky Mountains, and the Apache had vanished eastward like smoke in the wind. Father Domínguez left El Paso on March 1, 1776, with his secretary,

Father Palacio, and a second traveling companion, Father Peralta. They arrived in Santa Fe three weeks later. Almost immediately Domínguez began his inspections north of Santa Fe. What he found was disturbing.

Some of the missions had become little more than fortresses with the friars refusing to venture out unless they were given a military escort — a request seldom granted. He found situations where mission lands had fallen into the hands of neighboring ranchers. He discovered buildings in extreme levels of decay. Yet it was some of the priests themselves that disturbed Domínguez the most. The Franciscan order had been established on strict concepts of poverty, charity and chastity — practices Domínguez often found lacking. He discovered that priests had, for years, charged fees for performing marriages, baptisms and burials. Often these fees were so high that many Indian converts were barely able to pay. Even Spanish settlers had been forced to support the financial appetites of greedy priests.

To compound the problem he found record keeping a shambles. In his report he wrote, *"In a single mission I found the books of Marriages and Burials without a single entry recorded in them for a period of five years."* In one instance he noted that only the bindings of these books had been available, the pages they once contained had been cut out by various priests and used to roll cigarettes. Concerning the required mission schools he wrote, *"There is no teaching of the Indians and consequently no care taken to have them attend catechism and learn it."*

As for the concept of chastity he wrote that some of the friars carry on *" . . . with women who are not only suspect but leading notoriously evil lives."* He even named names. *"Father Salas lives all the whole week in the house of a married woman at whose side he goes night and day before the eyes of the whole pueblo."*

3

He also found priests who had overstepped their authority. *"Father Terán leads an unruly life, trading at the cost of the Indians' sweat, . . . and is so valiant that Captain of Militia don Miguel Espinosa is on his way to Chihuahua to tell the Caballero Inspector about the drubbing with a stick the said father gave him."*

Domínguez also found priests too old and frail to actively carry out their duties, and others who were forced to spend long hours each week in the saddle caring for the needs of their parishioners.

The missions south of Santa Fe were more in keeping with what Father Domínguez had expected to find. Albuquerque, sixty miles south of Santa Fe, had been founded by Spanish settlers in 1706. During the summers small fields of grain ripened beneath cloudless skies. Orchards of apricots, peaches and pears produced rich harvests. The mission church was unimposing but widely known for its hospitality to travelers. When Domínguez inspected its records he found that an entire volume had been filled with the records of marriages, births and baptisms. While the community was well-off and thriving, the church was showing considerable wear.

The two small bells meant to call worshippers for services were broken, vestments and even a large oil painting of Saint Francis Xavier were all " . . . *in poor condition from age."* Still, the interior of the building was much richer than those of the Indian mission churches north of Santa Fe. There was even a baptismal font made of copper.

Domínguez was impressed by the frugality of the local priest who saw to it that all candle stubs were melted down and recast so that not a drop of wax was wasted. Fray Andrés Garcia was fifty-eight years old, thirty-nine years a missionary with thirty of those years spent on the frontier. The report Domínguez submitted made note that the aging man spent long hours in the saddle tending to the spiritual needs not only of his own parish, but those of three outlying ones as well — a flock totaling nearly 2,500 souls.

Situated thirteen miles north of Albuquerque, at the foot of the soaring Sandia Mountains was the Sandia Mission. The previous summer it had been attacked by Comanches. When the raiders departed they left thirty of the 300 inhabitants dead. The site had been occupied, abandoned and then occupied again. Its most recent resettlement had occurred in 1748 as a home for some 350 native people who had left their homes in northeastern Arizona. They had inherited a badly weathered mission church beneath whose floor lay the bones of a priest who had been killed nearly 175 years earlier. Domínguez noted that the building was in " . . . *deplorable condition.*" Despite earlier efforts to repair and stabilize the structure, the church remained unusable. For that reason the baptistery was used as a place of worship, and crowded within its walls was a simple adobe altar, a wooden confessional, one chair and a small carved statue of Saint Anthony. Inventory included a few vestments, three old coins and an iron crowbar.

The priest, Father José Medrano was a native of Mexico, thirty-five years of age, and had served the mission four years. His support came almost entirely from the generosity of nearby Spanish ranchers. His own impoverished parishioners had very little to give. Father Medrano had planted several fruit trees, but winter cold next to the mountain and a recent drought had killed them all. The garden the priest planted produced very little, and even his few scraggly grape vines could do no more than maintain a tenuous grasp on life. Domínguez was impressed with Father Medrano's dedication, cleanliness, and the efforts he made to keep the mission alive, especially under such trying circumstances. Nevertheless, Domínguez noted in his report that the entire district was a " . . . *bit of a wasteland . . . .*"

A few miles north of Sandia was the pueblo of Santo Domingo. The town's history paralleled that of Santa Fe. It had been established in 1607 as the ecclesiastical center for all the Franciscan missions of New Mexico. During the Indian revolt of 1680 three resident priests had been murdered within its walls, their bodies unceremoniously dumped by their killers into a hole dug beneath the earthen floor of the church. Then the roof had been set afire.

The church was rebuilt after the Spaniards returned. The grave was left undisturbed. A life-size statue of Saint Domingo had been placed behind the alter, surrounded by ornaments of silver and gold. Domínguez wrote that the mission compound had been built perilously close to the edge of the Rio Grande River, the church especially so. (Years later a spring flood washed the church and the bones beneath its floor down the Rio Grande River.) It was noted that the church records contained an almost equal mix of Indian and Spanish names. Instead of farming, the local residents relied more on flocks of sheep and herds of cattle.

Father Domínguez, although not finished with his inspections, committed his findings to paper and dispatched the documents to his superiors in Mexico City. He had no way of knowing that his reports had set into motion complaints by the very priests he had named as being in error. Their defense was to suggest that a good or bad report depended on their willingness to provide Domínguez with a bribe. For the moment he knew nothing of that. His newest concern was to devote time to planning the expedition to California. It was already June. No one knew how long the trip might be, and he did not want to be stranded on the trail during winter. A departure date was set for July 4, 1776.

The governor of New Mexico, Don Pedro Fermín de Mendinueta, and several of his friends, had agreed to finance the expedition. They had no other choice. No funds had been sent north from Mexico City. Mendinueta had no intention of arousing the displeasure of his superiors, and the cost would be minimal. Horses were plentiful and cheap. Three months of supplies, trade goods, and pay for a handful of men would bankrupt no one. If the expedition proved successful there might even be recognition for those who funded the venture.

While these preparations were underway, Domínguez, still in Santa Fe, selected his second in command. A few weeks previous he had met a young priest from the Zuñi Mission which marked the western limits of the mission stations. Silvestre Vélez de Escalante had not been involved in any of the unsavory activities engaged in by some of his fellow Franciscans. He was a well-educated twenty-four year old native of Spain who had already established himself as a seasoned explorer and an excellent record keeper. He had traveled a considerable distance west of Zuñi the previous year learning what he could about both the land and the people.

What he had discovered was not encouraging. Indians he encountered had warned him about fierce warriors further west who ate the flesh of their victims, and in whose homeland flowed a mighty river imprisoned in the depths of a seemingly impassable gorge. Father Domínguez ordered the younger priest to join him in Santa Fe during the first week of June.

Preparations continued. The expedition still needed a map maker and navigator. Captain Don Bernardo Miera Y Pacheco was a retired Spanish artillery officer and a captain in the Santa Fe militia. In his mid-fifties he had expressed a keen interest in accompanying Father Domínguez, as he possessed many of the skills that would be needed for the expedition. Miera knew that Monterey Bay lay somewhere between the 37th and 38th degree of latitude. He suggested that if the expedition went north of Santa Fe 150 miles and then turned due west, it would be almost directly in line with the California colony. The captain had another reason for wanting to go north. Stories had long circulated about a navigable water route that led from somewhere in the interior of the continent to the western coast. He was convinced that if it did exist, a more northerly route for the expedition would provide a better opportunity for its discovery.

The days of June passed but as the July departure date came and went, supplies and animals that had been promised were still not available. To complicate matters Escalante fell gravely ill and remained so for nearly two weeks. Domínguez had no choice but to wait. It was just as well.

A day or so after the expedition had been scheduled to depart a letter arrived from Zuñi. It was from another explorer, Francisco Garcés, a Franciscan priest who had been involved in opening the land route along the west Mexican coast north to the colony of San Diego. With one Indian companion Garcés had traveled east through Arizona during the early summer of 1776. The two men passed the south rim of the Grand Canyon, at one point peering into its depths. They made it as far west as northeastern Arizona where, worn out and facing increasing Indian hostility, the priest penned a letter explaining the difficulties he had encountered in his journey. Garcés warned in his letter that the route he had taken, while passable, would not support the passage of supply trains or parties of immigrants. The land was mostly desert, water was difficult to find, forage for livestock almost non-existent and there was the matter of the canyon he had encountered. He persuaded a friendly Indian to carry his letter east and place it in the hands of the first Spaniard he came in contact with. Garcés had no way of knowing that he was only 100 miles from Zuñi. The letter reached Escalante's fellow priest at the Zuñi mission who immediately sent it on to Santa Fe.

As a result of the letter Miera was more convinced than ever that the expedition should travel north then west and so it was agreed. A guide was found who claimed to be familiar with at least the first 150 miles of the journey. The livestock and supplies were ready and after two weeks of rest, Escalante was ready to ride.

Chapter 2

WEST TO
⩔ CALIFORNIA ⩔

The morning sun had already appeared above the mountains east of Santa Fe. Forty horses and mules stamped and shuffled nervously in the plaza outside the Palace of the Governors. On the south side of the open square a small crowd emerged from the military chapel, The Church of Our Lady of Light. A special Mass and communion had just ended and the protection of God had been asked for a journey of exploration across the uncharted regions that lay between Santa Fe and the newly established Spanish missions in California. Ten men settled into their saddles and turned their mounts to the west side of the plaza. Leading the procession were two Franciscan priests. A captain of the Santa Fe militia followed, and behind him were four men leading the pack animals. The final three riders trailed the loose stock.

At the northern edge of town the expedition picked up a small collection of bawling cattle — enough to provide meat on the hoof for a three month journey. It was Monday, July 29, 1776. As the riders made their way northward along the Rio Grande River, they passed small fields of oats, barley, wheat, corn, onions, peas, melons, beans, a variety of fruit trees, and verdant gardens already showing a glint of red from ripening chili peppers. Water gurgled through grass-lined irrigation ditches. The morning air was heavy with the scent of piñon smoke from cooking fires. Children watched the expedition from yards splashed with the blooms of dahlias and oleanders brought north from the former empire of the Aztecs. West of the valley the spectacular Jemez Mountains stood against the morning sky, rich with forest lands and home to great flocks of sheep. Hidden from view, but some miles to the east, was the rugged Sangre de Cristo Range, higher than the Jemez, and stretching as far north as the eye could see. Millions of rolling acres stood between the two ranges, desert-like but rich enough in grass to provide grazing for still more flocks of shaggy Churro sheep, cattle and horses. The Rio Grande Valley had been Spain's northernmost colony for nearly 175 years, and while it had produced only limited amounts of silver and gold, local inhabitants lived comfortable lives sustained by what they took from the land.

Santa Fe's primary market and supply point was Chihuahua, 600 miles to the south. Thousands of sheep were sent along this route each year to help supply the meat markets of northern Mexico. Woolen blankets were also exported to Chihuahua. Traders returned to the northern colonies with coffee, sugar, chocolate, textiles, gunpowder and metal goods.

The area in and around Santa Fe had been explored by Spain as early as 1539, and by 1583 Spaniards were actively trading with Indian pueblos in the region. In 1598 more than 400 Spanish settlers made an arduous six month journey north out of Mexico bringing with them much of what they would need for settling the northern frontier, including a considerable assortment of livestock. They were accompanied by ten Franciscan friars who saw to it that one of the first permanent buildings constructed was a church. By 1610 the settlement was thriving. It was the mission priests who named it *La Villa Real de la Santa Fe de San Francisco de Assisi* — The Royal City

11

of the Holy Faith of Saint Francis of Assisi. Locals soon shortened it to Santa Fe.

As time passed, the native people who had been friendly and helpful during the first years of Spanish settlement grew increasingly restless and withdrawn. Spanish authorities had instituted a repressive system of taxation and work levies against their Indian neighbors. Priests had found it easier to convert by decree rather than by persuasion. Then, in 1680, in a burst of united fury, the Indian people of the Rio Grande Valley threw off the Spanish yoke.

The pueblos up and down the river revolted, and killed hundreds of Spaniards and their families as well as many of the priests. Santa Fe itself was placed under siege but the victorious Indians allowed the city to evacuate. The refugees streamed towards the closest secure Spanish settlement 260 miles south at El Paso. Soon afterward the united victory for the pueblo people disintegrated into disunity and factional squabbles. These events did not go unnoticed by the Spanish, and again the imperial colors of Spain marched north.

Spanish control of the region was regained, helped not a small amount, by Indian beliefs that recent drought and other turmoil had been the result of turning away from the God of the Spaniards. There would be no more talk about revolt, and the Spanish themselves returned with a less heavy-handed attitude.

Even in the missions there was change. Priests allowed their Indian converts to integrate some of their own customs and beliefs into that of the Church. The Franciscans began to challenge secular officials by siding with the Indians in matters of civil law. Even so, many Spaniards retained the belief that the Indian population was beneath them — little more than a class of servants. Santa Fe and the surrounding region grew, and almost a century after the ill-fated revolt, the Rio Grande Valley counted a non-Indian population of nearly

7,000 people. About that time, events far to the west began to unfold that would soon involve Santa Fe.

Spain had been aware of the existence of California for decades, but nothing had been done to encourage settlement of the region. Contrary winds and unpredictable ocean currents made sailing north along the Pacific coast treacherous, and no one had yet attempted to determine if an inland route might be opened to the region. Sea captains reported that much of what they saw beyond the coast appeared to be little more than desert.

In the early 1760s both Russian and English vessels began to explore the California coastal waters. It was feared that Russia intended to establish colonies, so against that possibility Spain's King Charles III gave his approval to establish Spanish settlements along the California coast. A series of missions was planned that would extend from the Bay of San Diego north to the Bay of Monterey, a zone of control that would stretch along more than 400 miles of coastline.

Three ships left Mexico in 1768 and sailed north towards San Diego. Separated by storms, one ship made its entrance into the bay after 54 days, the second in 110 days. The third vessel was never seen again. Meanwhile the Spanish sent 100 men overland. This party of soldiers, stock handlers, priests and Indians reached San Diego May 14, 1769, after a harrowing desert journey that had been plagued with accidents and illnesses. What was worse, the expedition arrived out of supplies and near starvation — a condition the new colony of San Diego was also facing. Local Indians showed no desire to assist the colonists. It was only through the timely arrival of an additional supply ship that the settlers avoided disaster.

In spite of these hardships, authorities in Mexico City were determined that settlement would proceed. On May 31, 1770,

Monterey was claimed as the northern most colony — further compounding the problems of supply. Explorers worked their way overland north from Mexico, and after four years of searching, had marked a trail that led North along the Colorado River then west towards the coast. The route contained adequate water and forage for stock. It was first crossed in late 1775, by a party of 250 immigrants from Mexico and their animals. One woman died and 100 head of livestock was lost — but three babies were born during the journey and they survived.

The trail held promise but many believed there had to be an easier route. Soldier and explorer, Juan Bautista de Anza had a theory. Santa Fe lay approximately 150 miles south of the Bay of Monterey in terms of latitude. It might be easier, he surmised, to reach the coast by that route. He was convinced enough to ride 1,600 miles south to Mexico City and there he persuaded authorities to mount an exploration party that would travel west from Santa Fe. Father Domínguez was selected to lead the expedition and to inspect the New Mexico missions at the same time.

Domínguez and his men covered 24 miles that July day of 1776 and made evening camp outside the Santa Clara Indian Pueblo. The following day, still traveling northwest, they covered an equal distance before reaching the frontier outpost of Abiquiú, built on a hillside south of the Chama River. There the party spent one day adjusting packs, checking gear and enjoying the hospitality of the town's 136 residents. On the morning of August 1, 1776, Domínguez and Escalante performed a joint Mass in the frontier post's simple but elegant little church. Afterwards the expedition moved west along the Chama River bordered with twisting, wooded canyons and high, rugged mesas. Abiquiú marked the end of the established trail and the beginning of the wilderness. It was at this time that Andrís Muñíz took the lead.

"We . . . arrived at . . . El Pueblo de Santa Rosa de Abiquiú, where . . . we once more implored the aid of our thrice-holy saints."
July 30, 1776.

Muñíz was an Indian from the Bernalillo Pueblo southwest of Santa Fe who was as comfortable with the Hispanic culture as he was with his own. Though he was less than thirty years old he was a self-made trader who had traveled north with earlier parties of explorers and traders, and was fluent in the Ute language — a tongue this expedition expected to need during much of their journey. Andrís brought with him his brother, Antonio Lucredio Muñíz. Antonio lacked the experiences of his older brother but he was a good stock tender, and an experienced packer. It was he who helped cover the packs that afternoon with tarps of linseed oil-painted canvas before a mid-afternoon thunderstorm drenched the area.

Three other Spaniards rounded out the expedition. Don Joaquín Laín had previously been living in Zuñi, Lorenzo Oliveres had come from El Paso, and Juan De Aguilar lived south of Albuquerque. Two priests, one middle aged soldier, four adventurers and three Hispanicized Indians — an unlikely team, yet they shared much common ground. Each man was at home on horseback as much as he was on foot. All had extensive experience living and surviving in the arid southwest, and each man knew that his chances to avoid death or injury might well depend on the man he rode next to. As for the leaders, Both Domínguez and Escalante were seasoned travelers, hardened to physical discomfort. They also provided spiritual insurance. No believer wanted to face death without first being administered the last rites of the Church, and only a priest could do that.

The second day of August the expedition turned north through a heavily wooded canyon. Four loose horses temporarily disappeared into the thick oak brush to graze, and had to be brought back by the stock tenders. Chokecherries ripened nearby as did lemita berries — a tart red berry used to make a drink similar to lemonade. There were also pea-sized manazanita berries, white when ripe, having a bittersweet but otherwise pleasant taste.

The riders temporarily left the bed of the river because of the increasingly thick vegetation they were encountering. Scrub oak gave way to open pastures and the men agreed that the grass was rich enough to support considerable numbers of horses and cattle.

The following morning the party made its way back to the

"The El Río de Chama . . . river ford is good, but on the margins nearby there are big hidden sinkholes."

Aug. 3, 1776.

banks of the Chama River. Andrís picked out a crossing point. The mayor of Zuñi, Don Pedro Cisneros, a friend of Escalante, selected his own crossing a few dozen yards upstream. The river was shallow, but both horse and rider disappeared into a hidden sink hole. The pair resurfaced, flailing the water as the horse struggled to regain solid footing. Cisneros had the presence of mind to maintain a tight grip on his musket. His servant Simón Lucero, a young Indian from Zuñi, retrieved his hat as it floated by. Still sputtering and gasping, the Spaniard rode up onto the bank. Someone began laughing, and soon others joined in. It was not recorded if the dripping Cisneros shared in the humor of his unexpected bath.

During the late afternoon, long after Cisneros was dry and the incident at the Chama River had been put aside, the party passed through a tangled, dense stand of pine. By this time lead ropes had been put away, and the pack animals were

"We set westward . . . along the box channel of El Rio de Chama."
Aug. 1.

traveling one behind the other. The cattle brought up the rear, trailed by two or three riders. Visibility was no more than a few feet. At times the pack train and loose horses were stretched out over more than a hundred yards. A loaded mule disappeared off into the brush unseen by anyone. It was not missed until they made camp that evening, but within a short time the animal appeared, eager to be freed of its load, and anxious to rejoin its companions.

"Don Bernardo Miera had been having stomach trouble all along and this afternoon he got much worse."

Aug. 6.

In six days the expedition had traveled 100 miles northwest of Santa Fe, and was 25 miles south of the future city of Pagosa Springs. On the banks of the Navajo River the expedition stopped in a mature stand of aspen, interspersed with patches of wild gooseberries and chokecherry. Escalante made note that the region had potential for a good-sized settlement. Domínguez had called for a temporary halt to allow Miera time to work on his map and take a latitude reading with his astrolabe. The captain's calculations indicated that they were still south of the line that passed through Monterey Bay. Certain that the great canyon and possible hostile Indians lay directly in their path, the expedition leaders decided they would continue towards the northwest. Miera up-dated his map but was suffering from steadily increasing stomach pains. He decided that he found more comfort in the saddle than on the ground, so the expedition continued on and rode until sunset. By the next morning his ailment had disappeared.

As the party passed along the future Colorado/New Mexico border the men could see that with irrigation, not one but several future settlements might be built. Hay meadows were extensive, and grass grew verdantly on the surrounding hillsides. As they climbed out of a winding canyon they could see, to the north, the soaring heights of the La Plata Mountains — still wearing a summer mantle of snow. Andrís Muñíz told the group they would travel around the high peaks and not through them. His words were taken with a certain disappointment. Several of the expedition members had hoped to do a little prospecting along the way, as the name *plata* meant silver.

An uneventful day drifted by as the party rode through more lands rich with potential for settlement. During late afternoon they crossed the Animas River and began a gradual climb to the west, the flanks of the hills emerald green with grass. The men examined exposed rock ledges. Earlier explorers had written about metallic ores they had found west of the Animas but, this day, no one found anything of interest. As the expedition climbed higher the air turned cooler, and riders found an abundance of ripe wild berries that they picked from the saddle. Late that afternoon it began to rain — cold, heavy drops driven by a stinging wind. The men protected themselves with tightly woven ponchos they kept draped across the fronts of their saddles. Woven from two strips of lanolin rich wool two feet wide and eight feet long, the pieces were sewn together with a hole left in the middle for the wearer's head to fit through. The garments were woven tightly enough to deflect wind as well as rain, and also made up part of a traveler's sleeping gear.

It proved difficult to find dry wood that night, as intermittent showers continued. By morning Domínguez was suffering from a severe sinus problem. The jarring he would receive from riding would be nothing less than torture. The group decided to allow him to rest and to let the stock graze for the day.

"We did not proceed ahead today because the mounts had not fed enough the night before . . . and also because of a thick and prolonged heavy downpour."

Aug. 9.

The following morning, although the priest was no better and intermittent rain continued, the party broke camp and headed in a more northerly direction. Hampered by the wet, slippery ground and Domínguez' condition, the expedition made early camp along the banks of a small creek. Miserable and wet, men huddled beneath what shelter they could find or make. Daybreak brought more downpours and it was decided that there would be no travel that day.

Daybreak, August 12, brought clearing skies, and although Domínguez was feverish and having difficulties breathing, he insisted that they move on. Despite the mud, the expedition was able to cover twenty-two miles over flat, easy terrain. Camp was made within sight of present-day Dolores. That night Domínguez' condition worsened so it was decided the next morning not to break camp. Miera took another latitude reading and worked on his map while Domínguez rested. Escalante and several of the expedition members spent the day exploring. On a hilltop west of camp they found the tumbled-in ruins of what they believed to be an ancient Indian pueblo. What the men did not know was they were the first Europeans to see ancient Anasazi

"Upon an elevation . . . there was in ancient times a small settlement."
Aug. 13. Escalante Ruin west of Dolores, CO.

dwellings. They were only a day's ride north of the massive ruins at Mesa Verde.

A new dawn painted the eastern skyline and Domínguez proclaimed he was well enough to ride. Andrís continued to lead them northwest over rolling hills reminiscent of ocean swells in the aftermath of a storm, frozen forever in a moment of time. Scattered groves of piñon and juniper grew among the rock strewn slopes. Then, after ten miles the hills began to level out and two distant mountains appeared. Andrís kept the riders pointed towards the northernmost peak. Thick stands of giant sagebrush replaced the scattered groves of trees, making travel more difficult. The men rode almost to the present town of Dove Creek, then turned due north.

By early afternoon on the fourteenth of August, two riders appeared from the south and began to close the gap between themselves and the expedition. The party stopped, waiting as the horsemen drew closer. Hesitantly two men rode within a few feet of Escalante, stopped, dismounted, approached and removed their hats. Felipe, of mixed Spanish and Indian blood, spoke for both himself and his companion Juan Domingo, an Indian from a tribe Escalante could not determine. The two men had been stock tenders at a ranch near Abiquiú. They had stolen horses and supplies and had followed the expedition for almost two weeks. When they were certain they were not being pursued they made their appearance. Filipe asked if they might join. Escalante looked at Domínguez but the expedition leader indicated that this decision was in the hands of his second in command.

"This afternoon we were overtaken by a coyote and a genízaro from Abiquiú, the first Filipe and the second Juan Domingo by name."

Aug. 14.

For a moment the young priest weighed the situation. If he ordered the men back to Abiquiú they would disappear into the wilderness and very likely connect with friendly Indians. Who knew what mischief that might cause? It was no great crime to take a horse. Many ranchers could not even identify much of their own stock. Stealing a few supplies could hardly be counted as a jailable offense — even if there had been a jail in Abiquiú. Besides, who could say that these men were not justified in leaving a situation where they received little more than food and a place to sleep? It would do no harm to have two additional stock tenders. The moments ticked by. Heads bowed slightly, but with pleading eyes lifted towards the priest, Filipe and Juan Domingo waited. Finally,

Escalante made the decision Saint Francis himself probably would have made. They could come along, but Escalante made it clear he would tolerate no idleness from the two runaways, and they would do penance for their sins.

The party, now numbering twelve, continued through dense sagebrush. Numerous times they had to backtrack when brush became too thick to ride through, and the formerly confident Andrés began to appear confused. For the first time in more than two and a half weeks into their journey he could not find water. A hot August sun burned down and the loose stock that trailed the riders had

"We discovered more than half of the horses missing, since, having had no water, they strayed away."

Aug. 16.

begun to grow restless. The two newest members eagerly added their efforts to keeping the animals in the line of march. Other riders fanned out to search for pools that might be left in deep washes from the recent rains. They found only enough for the men, nothing for the stock. During the night of August 16, more than half the thirsty horses and mules wandered off in the darkness. They were found late the next morning still lingering by the muddy pool of water they had found. The rest of the stock was brought in and allowed to drink. By then it was late afternoon and too late to travel more than a few miles.

Captain Miera, agitated by the indecisiveness of Andrés, had ridden off alone some hours earlier. His tracks pointed northeast — towards the rugged Dolores Canyon. One man was sent ahead to follow Miera while Domínguez questioned

Andrés Muñíz about the route ahead. The answers he received were not encouraging. It was obvious that the guide had lost his way. It was also evident that travel any further west risked losing animals to thirst. Perhaps Captain Miera had the right idea — enter the Dolores Canyon and head downstream towards the north and hope that the river would eventually turn towards the west. The expedition remounted and followed Miera's tracks.

Chapter 3

FINDING A
GUIDE

The expedition rode into the first hours of evening before making camp. There, in the gathering darkness they waited. Neither Miera nor the man who had been sent after him had returned. Campfires were finally banked for the night and everyone rolled into their blankets, except Domínguez and Escalante. The priests remained awake and kept one fire burning — a hopeful beacon. Their efforts were rewarded near midnight. Tired but ecstatic, Miera and his companion related how they had found a way to the canyon floor of the Dolores River. The two expedition leaders listened, but said nothing about Miera's hot-tempered disappearance that previous afternoon. Dawn was less than three hours away when the four men finally slept.

At sunup Captain Miera took the lead as the expedition wound its way down into the depths of the canyon. The thirsty animals needed no prodding. They could smell the water. Then, at the river's edge, one of the men gave a yell. Pressed into the wet sand by the water's edge were fresh moccasin imprints pointing up stream. Andrés assured the padres that these had to be tracks of friendly Utes. Domínguez, Cisneros and Andrés turned their horses upstream in pursuit of the tracks. These might well be people who knew the way out of the canyon. For a mile or so the prints showed no particular hurry, then suddenly lengthened into running strides. The Spaniards had apparently been spotted, and the track makers were showing no indication they wanted to make contact. The three riders picked up their own pace but they soon lost the trail in the rocks. There was nothing to do but turn their mounts and rejoin their companions.

The main expedition found the going easy the first mile but after that the canyon began to narrow. The river twisted and turned like the death throes of a dying serpent. Narrow sand bars along the banks were littered with rock that had fallen from the cliffs and footing for the animals became increasingly difficult. Only by crossing and recrossing the stream were they able to continue. The day lengthened as men and animals picked their way through rocks, sand and water. Horses slipped and stumbled. Cattle bawled in protest as sharp stones left cuts and gashes on their legs. At one point a narrow path appeared that led up and out of the east side of the canyon. East was not the direction the expedition wanted to go so the party struggled on. That night, camped on a narrow shelf next to the water, both men and animals slept the sleep of exhaustion. The entire day's journey had gained them less than three miles through the gorge.

"Two of the companions . . . returned about eight in the morning, saying that only through the river's box channel could we get out."

Aug. 19.

At first light scouts were sent further downstream to look for a way out. They returned two hours after sunup and reported an exit down river leading up the west wall. It would be a very difficult climb that led into a maze of rock shelves near the rim. It was doubtful that all the animals would make it. If even one lost its footing and fell, it might well sweep those behind it to their deaths on the canyon floor. If the path could be successfully negotiated it was almost certain that it would lead the expedition back to the waterless desert lands west of the gorge. Consideration returned to the trail up the east wall of the canyon, the one that

"We conferred with the companions who had journeyed through this region as to which direction we should take . . . and each one had a different opinion."

Aug. 19.

had been discovered the previous day. The scouts were certain it would be a much easier way out except that it went the wrong direction. Each man was given a chance to voice his opinion, east or west, but there was no consensus. Finally, it was decided to put the decision in God's hands through a casting of lots. Two sticks were marked, one indicating the trail leading west to the desert country, the other to whatever lay to the east. Both priests prayed and an expedition member drew one of the sticks. After several hours of torturous backtracking the expedition was at the base of the east trail.

The climb out proved more difficult than anticipated, especially for the cattle, but eventually the men and animals stood on the rim, freed from the serpentine depths of the Canyon of the Dolores. Unfortunately, the battle was not over. The east canyon rim was also lined with a series of rock shelves similar to those on the west side. Again the struggling animals left blood on the stones. At long last the ground evened out, and the riders found themselves on a well-used Indian trail that pointed towards the northeast. It was not the direction they wished to go but no one argued. God alone had made the decision which trail to take.

That evening camp was pitched at an abandoned Indian campsite which contained both water and forage to fill the bellies of the exhausted animals. They had put sixteen miles between themselves and the canyon exit. For the moment their route to the west was blocked by the canyon — how far, there was no way of knowing. They desperately needed to find someone who knew. For the time being they felt that they had to remain on the Indian trail that continued towards the northeast.

By the end of the following day they made camp along the banks of the San Miguel River. Ahead of them lay the gently rising heights of the Uncompahgre Plateau. The trail they were on was easy to follow and obviously well used. The expedition leaders were hoping that it would soon lead them to friendly Utes.

"We traveled north four leagues of very good terrain."
Aug. 21. One day after leaving Dolores Canyon.

On the morning of August 22, the party saddled up and began to wind upwards through scattered stands of juniper and piñon. The air became cooler. Animals paused periodically to snatch at clumps of grass. The pace remained leisurely and even the cantankerous Miera seemed not to mind. It was beautiful country. To the southeast lay the massive and jagged walls of the San Juan Mountains. The pointed tops of the La Sal range could be seen along the northwest horizon. Below and to the right ran the waters of the San Miguel in a channel choked and tangled with vegetation and water-polished stones. The riders passed the tumbled down stone walls of either a former home or perhaps a fortification. Less than a mile later an Indian stepped from behind a large rock — staring intently at the Spaniards. Every rider stopped. Andrés the interpreter called out in the Ute tongue and the man answered back. He wished to talk.

The two priests and the interpreter approached the Ute warrior with a gift of tobacco and food. The rest of the party kept their distance, fearful that any wrong move might provoke the man into flight. After the Indian had accepted the gifts, Andrés

"We were overtaken by a Tabehuachi Yuta. We gave him something to eat and to smoke, and afterwards . . . asked him . . . about the land ahead."

Aug. 23.

asked if there were others nearby. The man's answer was deliberately vague. Andrés explained that the expedition needed a guide and would be willing to pay whoever could lead them west. One of the priests suggestively held out two steel knives and several strings of white glass beads. The warrior's eyes darted from face to face searching for treachery. Finally he agreed — not to lead the party west, but rather further north to a Ute summer camp. Perhaps there they could find the guide they wanted. If the expedition made camp and waited for him, he would return the following morning. Without waiting for an answer he took to his feet and disappeared through the boulders and trees.

The men made camp and daylight faded into darkness. Would the visitor keep his word or would he lead a war party into the camp at dawn? Years previously Ute raiders had attacked the settlement at Abiquiú. It had been a bloody affair where men, women and children had died. There was little sleep that night.

Apprehension melted away only when the Ute reappeared shortly after sunup bringing with him two women and five children. Two were infants and the remaining three ranged from eight to ten years of age — wide-eyed and intensely curious about the strangely dressed men with hair on their faces. The women spread a tanned deer skin on the ground and poured out two small piles of dried raisin-like manzanita berries and beside that, a small quantity of dried deer meat. They wanted the white flour that made bread. A trade was made and afterwards the warrior began to talk.

He was in no particular hurry and conversation continued through most of the morning. He was asked if he had heard of a Spanish priest and explorer from the west named Garcés? He had not. At noon a meal of campfire bread was provided for the warrior, the women and the wide-eyed children. It was obvious they were pleased. When the meal had been eaten the warrior indicated it was time to leave. He would lead the party on a four day journey north to a summer camp of Utes, then he would return to his family. He wanted his pay in advance. Domínguez presented him with two steel butcher knives and sixteen strings of white glass beads, all of which he immediately turned over to the older woman. Clutching the treasures tightly, she disappeared through the shadows of the trees, followed by her companion and the brood of children.

The expedition mounted up behind their new guide. Escalante named him Atanasio, in honor of Domínguez, and for the remainder of the afternoon he led them down the east flank of the Uncompahgre Plateau still following the well-defined path which, at one point, separated into three branches. Atanasio took the one to the far left and by sunset the party arrived at a campsite with a spring of cold, sweet water. Ample grass grew among the aspen and there was dry firewood. That night there was sleep.

The morning sun was squarely in their eyes as the party continued to wind way down the plateau towards a broad valley that stretched far to the north. On the northern horizon they could see what appeared to be a wall of rock, a mesa of incredible size, a flat topped mountain.

Dark, swollen clouds came in from the southwest and camp was made early, but an increasingly heavy rain made the cooking fires hiss, sputter and die before they could be put to use. Rain continued off and on throughout much of the night. Jagged flashes of lightning touched the southern peaks, each time followed by rumbling peals of thunder. It was almost as though the mountains themselves were talking. The men, wet and miserable, finally saw the stars an hour before the dawn of August 26.

Despite the rain of the previous night the rocky ground gave firm footing. The trail forked once more and for a second time Atanasio took the one to the left. Six miles later the expedition halted on the west bank of the Uncompahgre River. Their guide explained that many miles up-stream, hot springs,

"We . . . came upon the banks of . . . Ancapagari which . . . means Red Lake, because . . . near its source there is a spring of red-colored water, hot and ill-tasting."

Aug. 26.

red in color, mingled with the cold waters of the river. Each summer, after high waters had subsided, bathers would build barricades of stones to mix the waters of the hot springs with those of the stream. They called their soaking pool "Uncompahgre" — hot red water standing.

An hour before the sun dipped below the western ridges, they camped near a marsh — on the present grounds of the Ute Indian Museum on the south end of modern day Montrose. Escalante spent the evening writing in the expedition journal. What he had seen in the Uncompahgre Valley excited him. *"It abounds with good pasturages and is very moist and has good lands for farming without irrigation. Here it has a meadow of good land for farming with the help of irrigation."* He was in awe of the massive peaks of the San Juans which lay to the south and the jagged ridges that walled the southeastern end of the valley. He made note of the desolate, leaden colored hills of shale to the east. To the north Escalante could now more easily see the dark, brooding heights of Grand Mesa, its western end, like the prow of an ancient ship, pointing suggestively towards California. That evening the expedition dined on grouse, spitted on sticks of green willow and roasted over beds of piñon coals.

Next morning they continued down river, keeping to the west bank where they met another Ute Indian and his family. An attempt at conversation yielded nothing. The man would not even converse with their new guide, Atanasio. The

"We . . . halted next to a big marsh greatly abounding in pasturage . . . ."

Aug. 26. Expedition campsite on the grounds of the Ute Indian Museum in Montrose.

expedition rode on and, in jest, the expedition members referred to the Ute they had met as *"the deaf one."* The day grew hot and, south of the present site of Olathe, the Uncompahgre River broke into a series of vegetation-choked channels. Atanasio led them across a ford to the east bank where the downstream trail picked up again. That evening they camped on a grassy flat north of Olathe.

Andrés had regained his bearings and explained to Escalante that less than ten miles down river, near where the Uncompahgre joined the Gunnison, the previous expedition he had been on had camped and carved a cross and other identifying marks in a young cottonwood before turning back towards Santa Fe. What lay beyond that cross — he did not know.

The next morning their Indian guide led the party away from the river to the northeast and across a series of heat-soaked adobe hills. It was difficult traveling. Dust swirled and horse hooves sunk into the powdery Mancos shale. By early afternoon the expedition had crossed the Gunnison River and shortly afterwards was camped in a well-grassed flat east of the town of today's Austin. Atanasio and Andrés continued upriver in hopes of finding a Ute encampment.

The expedition had been on the trail a month now. Several horses were showing signs of fatigue, the expedition's ninety day food supply was declining at a precipitous rate and, according to a latitude reading taken by Miera, the expedition was now a hundred miles north of the route which would lead them straight west to Monterey. They also needed to find a new guide. Atanasio had fulfilled his agreement.

"Five Sabuagana Yutas let themselves be seen . . . to fill us with fear by exaggerating the danger to which we were exposing ourselves."

Aug. 29.

About ten in the morning on August 29, five Utes appeared on the brow of a hill above the camp. The visitors made signs of friendship then warily made their way down to the camp where they were fed and given gifts of tobacco. There was no interpreter present, but the Spaniards did understand one word — *Comanche*. It was a name which sent chills down the spines of the expedition members. Could it be possible the war parties that had plagued the New Mexico settlements the previous summer were this far north or could they be different ones? That evening the five Utes left the camp and returned over the ridge from which they had first appeared, leaving the question unanswered.

The following morning Andrés and Atanasio returned with five different Utes and one boy. The new arrivals were given food and tobacco. One of the steers from the beef herd was killed and the Indians ate ravenously. Andrés had already explained to them that the expedition needed a new guide — one who could take the expedition west. Interest was piqued immediately when it was discovered one of the visitors and the boy claimed to be from a tribe much further to the west — they were Laguna Utes. Small talk continued. It was claimed that a passage directly west would be nearly impossible. The terrain was difficult and there would be little water. Severe drought of the previous few years had made many watering sites unreliable. It was explained that the expedition would have to travel further north before they could point their horses west. It would be necessary to cross the flank of Grand Mesa and then travel ten to twelve days northwest towards a crossing on the Green River. A series of trails west from the Green would lead the party to Utah Lake and the Lagunas. Mention was made of an even larger lake north of that, one whose waters were too salty to drink.

It was Miera's turn to show interest. This could be the fabled inlet from the Pacific. California might be closer than they thought.

Again the word *Comanche* came into the conversation. Miera surmised this might be the same band that wintered east of the Rocky Mountains north of the Arkansas River — the same warriors who had attacked the settlements the previous year. It was not uncommon for mounted Indians to range far from their camps to hunt or make war. The twelve Spaniards had no more than half a dozen muskets. If spotted they would have almost no chance against superior numbers of warriors armed with firearms and ammunition obtained from French traders to the east.

Comanches or not, Domínguez turned the conversation back to obtaining a guide. He offered a wool blanket, a steel butcher knife and several strands of beads to the Laguna Ute. The man's four companions began to argue that for such treasures they too would serve as guides. Domínguez was firm, he wanted one guide. The Utes decided the final decision would be made by a tribal council. Domínguez and Escalante were to visit the warriors' camp. It was early afternoon by the time the expedition was packed up and ready to move out. Atanasio, his agreement fulfilled, turned his horse southwest towards the Uncompahgre River and disappeared across the gray adobe hills.

With their new companions in the lead, the Spaniards rode almost due east through the valley of the north fork of the Gunnison River. As the terrain climbed they could see the uplift of the Black Canyon a few miles to the south. Its half mile deep gorge was hidden from their view but beyond lay mountains that covered the entire southern horizon. Somewhere beyond those peaks was Santa Fe. Various expedition members settled their gaze in the direction of home. The thoughts of another long detour and a Comanche ambush was very much on their minds.

That night they camped west of present-day Hotchkiss on the edge of a good pasture ringed with aspen and scrub oak. Once more they fed their Indian guests who ate until they could consume no more. Another day passed and the party turned to a northern heading, still following the river. Late in the afternoon they camped near the site of Bowie and killed another steer. The Indians feasted, gorging on the fresh beef. Afterwards, for better than an hour one of the warriors rolled on the ground clutching his midsection and wailing that he had been poisoned. Escalante wrote, *"One of the Sabuagana*

Yutas who accompanied us . . . ate with such brutish savagery that we thought he was going to die from overstuffing. But God willed that he recovered, after he vomited some of the great mass he could not digest. Today 24 miles."

" . . . *after going three leagues through narrow valleys of . . . thick clumps of scrub oak we came upon eighty Yutas.*
Sept. 1. Atop the east side of Grand Mesa.

The first day of September was sunny and cool. The expedition continued north up Hubbard Creek on the east end of Grand Mesa. Eight miles later they rode into a Ute camp of more than eighty men, women and children. The warriors were heavily armed and mounted on good horses. Andrés was told that the men were about to depart on a hunt. Was it a show of strength or did the Utes have something else in mind? It was decided that the expedition should ride on until they came to a place where they could make a reasonably defensible camp. Only the Laguna warrior from the west accompanied them.

After camp had been made Domínguez, Andrés and the Laguna rode back to the Utes. The men had not left to hunt but there was no longer an open display of weapons. Perhaps the Indians had been merely taking precautions. Domínguez gazed about him. Nearly 100 pairs of dark eyes stared back — expectantly. The issue of obtaining a guide could wait. This was an opportunity presented by heaven. The priest had a captive congregation.

With Andrés interpreting, Domínguez began a missionary sermon. It was short and simple, the essence of which Escalante preserved in the journal that night, *"Christ crucified — is the one Lord of all, who dwells in the highest part of the skies, and in order to please Him and go to Him one has to be baptized and must beg His forgiveness."* Andrés translated from Spanish to Ute but one older Indian, hard of hearing, asked that the words be repeated. The Laguna warrior from the west went to the old man's side and repeated each word in the Ute tongue. For emphasis he beat one fist against his chest. Domínguez watched. With the help of the Laguna, the priest held the rapt attention of his audience.

He talked about the differences between men and beasts. He spoke about the creation and the reason for man's life being to serve the living God. Domínguez asked the tribal elders to consider what had been said and if they were favorable, at a later time, he and Escalante would return to teach and baptize.

An old warrior then gave commands and a quantity of dried bison meat was brought out and offered for trade. Domínguez knew his time of preaching was over. He offered a quantity of beads for the meat and asked if an exchange might also be made of some of the Spaniard's trail-worn horses for some of those owned by the Utes. Additional trade goods would accompany any horse trades. The Utes were agreeable.

A short time later the priest and Andrés rode back to their camp. The Laguna remained behind. If nothing had come of the sermon at least they would be able to replace their weakest horses and there would be dried meat to include in their commissary packs. Their small herd of cattle was rapidly being depleted. The same could be said for their corn meal and flour. They had not counted on the extra mouths they had been feeding and California was still nearly as far away as it had been when they had left Santa Fe more than a month ago. It was fortunate that adequate trade goods were left. Surely there would be other Indians and the Spaniards could continue to barter for what they needed.

Near sundown a number of warriors, the Laguna Ute and several tribal elders came to the Spanish camp but they brought no spare horses. The conversation immediately took on an ominous tone. The tribal elders began by again warning the Spaniards about the Comanche threat to the north. They emphasized that these were people who would not allow the expedition to pass through their lands. References were made to specific kinds of torture a captive might expect. One warrior graphically went through the motions of slashing his chest cavity and wrenching out a living heart. Domínguez was not shaken, rather he steadfastly continued to insist that Comanches or not, the expedition would go on. The Ute elders replied that to do so would be foolish. The Spaniards were too lightly armed. Domínguez countered that the expedition's strength came not from arms but from the protection of God. The conversation was going in circles. Finally the Utes requested that the padres write a letter to the Spanish governor telling him that the expedition had passed through their country and that should the Spaniards meet with a disaster that it had not been the fault of the Grand Mesa Utes.

Something did not seem right but the request was granted and Domínguez said that the letter would be left with the tribal leaders. The Ute elders countered that this would not be satisfactory. They wanted the letter delivered to the governor by Andrés the interpreter and his brother Lucrecio. Domínguez shot a quick look at Escalante and Captain Miera. Suddenly the conversation began to make sense.

Andrés was led from the camp where he made a complete confession. More in fear for his immortal soul than his temporal body, the words tumbled out. Yes, the Comanche threat was real but he had added to the words of the Ute leaders. Andrés and Lucrecio had traveled far enough. They wanted to return to Santa Fe, alone and across the mountains if necessary. He and his brother had also broken one of the expedition rules by bringing along trade goods of their own, some of which they had already exchanged for bows and quivers of arrows in anticipation for the trip home. The expedition leaders were stunned. What else had he distorted? At that point they would have willingly given the two men their wish but the expedition needed someone who could translate the Ute language, and only Andrés had that ability. Escalante wrote later that, *"This caused us much grief and very much also that follows."* There was no more talk that evening at the council fire.

The Utes returned early the following morning. It was the second day of September. This time they presented a new argument. They did not want the Laguna Ute to accompany the expedition west even though the man had agreed to do so — an agreement already sealed with a bright red blanket, but with the treachery of Andrés no longer standing in the way, the intent of the Utes was becoming clear. It was not so much that they feared what might happen if the expedition ventured into Comanche lands, rather they did not want to lose this band of travelers with their tame cattle and packs of trade goods. When the tribal elders realized their arguments were falling on deaf ears they relented and agreed that the Laguna from Utah Lake was free to go as a guide, and that the promise of fresh horses would be honored.

Later that day the Spaniards moved out towards the northwest. They named their new guide Silvestre and gave him one of their own horses. At the last moment, impulsively almost, the Laguna boy they had met some days earlier appeared, running alongside the men. He too wanted to return to his

"The . . . brother of Chief Yamutzi, addressed the others and said that, since they had granted us passage . . . placing obstacles before us was no longer appropriate."

Sept. 2.

home near Utah Lake. Don Joaquín Laín laughingly reached down and pulled the lad up behind him. That night it rained heavily.

Through leaden skies of dawn the rain came again and the expedition was forced to make a late start. Silvestre said little but remained in the lead twisting and winding through forests of aspen already showing the first colors of autumn. The country did not lack for water or forage, and no longer slowed by the weaker animals they had traded, the miles passed by. They were still climbing but the ascent was gradual. Escalante made mention in the journal of the numerous and extensive beaver dams they saw, fifteen feet high in some cases. Old Indian campsites were plentiful and high on the mountain the riders encountered three Ute women and a child drying wild chokecherries and gooseberries. They had

"The gooseberry . . . is very sour on the bush, but when already exposed to the sun, as these Yuta women had it, it has a very delicious sweet-sour taste."

Sept. 4.

no fear of the Spaniards. It was assumed that they belonged to the band some miles back. A trade pack was opened and the women exchanged the berries they had already dried for a few strings of white beads.

The expedition turned west and continued down a grassy valley where camp was made nine miles west of the present site of Colbran. Golden aspen leaves quivered in the fading light while a chilly September wind blew from the northwest.

"The beavers have constructed ponds."

Sept. 4. On top of Grand Mesa

*"We . . . went up an incline without troublesome rocks but
extremely steep and dangerous when approaching the top."*
Sept. 5. Leaving the north end of Grand Mesa.

Clear skies greeted the dawn. Silvestre turned up a small
creek and headed north. It was a difficult trail that twisted and
wound its way up and over Battlement Mesa. Late in the
afternoon they stood on the banks of the Colorado River. The
guide picked a place to ford and the water nearly touched the
bottoms of the packs, cold, clear and swift. That night
Captain Miera took another latitude reading and calculated
the distance the expedition had traveled from Santa Fe. It had
been a twisting, torturous journey of 560 miles, and they were
only a little closer to California than when they had started.

The following day Silvestre led the party westward down
the river. Travel was easy and at last they were traveling in the
right direction. Then, near noon their guide turned them
away from the water and up a canyon that led almost directly
north. Riders reined in their mounts. Andrés spoke for a long

"The meridian was taken, and we found that we were at 41° 6' 53"
latitude."

Sept. 7. After crossing the Colorado River.
Detail from a wall mural at Paonia, CO. by Ginny Allen.

time with Silvestre who claimed that this was the route he was
familiar with. He did not know what lay directly to the west.
Suspicion flared. They had been told that the land to the
north was Comanche country. Was their guide leading them
into a trap? No one knew how far the river flowed west.
Perhaps it turned north or even south. It might well enter
another impassable canyon. The expedition had no choice
but to continue following the Laguna Ute — but they would
be watchful. The few muskets they had were kept primed.

That evening six Ute warriors approached the
Spaniards' camp. They said they had come from the east on a
raid against the Comanche who had left the mountains and
were headed for winter camps along the Arkansas River to the
southeast. If the report was true it was welcome news but

doubts remained. Comanche raiders often operated in groups independent of each other. There was no way of knowing if they had all departed.

For the next three days the riders continued towards the northwest. At times Silvestre set a course that passed through deep, winding ravines — excellent places for an ambush. Then he led them up steep, slide-prone hillsides to follow a ridge line. The Spaniards knew that, exposed on the skyline, they could be seen by a potential enemy for miles. Yet it was evident to the trail-wise Spaniards that Silvestre was picking the best route possible for the animals even though the men were frequently forced to dismount and lead their horses up and down the steep slopes.

On one occasion two loaded pack mules lost their footing on loose shale and rolled more than sixty feet down a

"We reached a high ridge where the guide Silvestre pointed out to us the sierra on whose northern side dwell the Yamparica Comanches."
Sept. 8. Near Douglas Pass in northwestern Colorado.

hillside but without serious injury. The land itself had become more barren. Water and forage were increasingly difficult to find. Guards had to be posted at night to keep hungry and thirsty animals from wandering away. On two occasions the expedition saw warlike figures and symbols painted on canyon walls but they looked like they had been there for a long time. Finally, the ravines and ridges ended as the weary, dust-covered travelers looked down on the White River. It flowed through a valley that appeared as desolate as the country they had just crossed. At least there was water for the stock and limited forage.

That night a disappointed Escalante wrote, *"This river is middling and flows west through here, and the terrain adjacent to it offers no prospects for a settlement. Today 26 miles."* It was one of the few times the young journal keeper was to be proven wrong in judging a potential settlement. He had no way of knowing about oil and natural gas. Today the town of Rangely occupies the site he referred to.

"Two pack mules lost their footing and rolled down more than twenty yards at the least . . . they came out unhurt."

Sept. 7.

"Halfway in this canyon toward the south there is a quite lofty rock cliff on which we saw, crudely painted, three shields . . . and a spearhead . . . we named it El Cañón Pintado."

Sept. 9.

Morning came and they moved on, away from the river and through yet another region devoid of water and grass. That night guards were posted to keep the stock from returning back to the waters of the White River.

Midway through the following morning Silvestre led them to a tiny spring, enough for the men but not enough for the stock. As they drank he promised a larger flow of water further on, enough for the animals. A short time later a mule collapsed. Its load was divided among the other pack animals and the weakened creature struggled along at the rear of the column, unwilling to be left behind. Late in the afternoon Silvestre's promise of water and adequate grass was fulfilled. The weakened mule was still with them.

For the expedition another problem was becoming more evident. The last beef animal had been killed and eaten days

"After going a league and a half through arroyos and embankments, . . . we found in one of them a tiny spring of water."
Sept. 11. West of Rangely, CO.

earlier and rations of flour, cornmeal and other basic food stuffs would be depleted in three or four weeks. For the past day, however, they had seen fresh signs of bison. It was decided to let the stock rest and send out a hunting party. Success came the next morning in the form of a large bison bull, chased down and shot before being cut into thin slices that were spread across bush tops to dry in the sun and wind. The meat was tough and stringy but it had a good flavor. By the evening of the following day the strips, now shriveled and black, were dry enough to pack away. That night it rained heavily for the first time since the party had left Grand Mesa. The men spent a wet night, glad their new supply of meat was safe and dry beneath water-resistant pack covers.

"One of them returned saying that they had found the bison . . . after chasing it about seven miles, they killed it . . . they brought back a grand supply of meat."

Sept. 11.

September 13 dawned clear and cool. The stock grazed late into the morning as the rain-slick ground firmed up beneath a warming sun. About noon the expedition mounted and Silvestre led them to a well-traveled trail near what would become the Colorado/Utah state line. Grass was more abundant and the riders rode by numerous springs and water holes. The trail they were on began to converge with others and their guide assured them that they would reach the next river by evening.

Near sunset Silvestre led the men to a meadow a mile or so below what he claimed was the only ford across the Green River for many day's journey either up or downstream. The

Spaniards could see that the man spoke the truth. The river emerged from a deep canyon, and swept around a bend where it deposited its load of gravel and small rocks. This made a level and solid bottom that animals could easily cross without sinking into the mud. The waters then slowed, and continued south to widen out and unload miles of quicksand that could quickly swallow up both horse and rider.

Camp was made in a small grove of cotton-woods six miles north of present day Jenson, Utah. Grass was abundant. It was time to rest and allow the animals to regain strength and flesh. Saturday, September 14, dawned free of clouds, and with a warming sun. While others busied themselves repairing gear

"Near its trunk, on the side facing northwest, Don Joaquín Laín . . . with a chisel carved . . . "Year of 1776," and . . . Laín *with two crosses at the sides."*

Sept. 14.

and doing camp chores, Don Joaquín Laín chopped away the bark on a nearby cottonwood and in the naked wood under-neath he carved the year, his name and two small crosses. Captain Miera took a latitude reading. For reasons he could not understand, the measurement did not correspond with earlier readings. That night he repeated the measurement, this time using the North Star, only to arrive at the same reading. He assumed that local conditions were affecting his compass. The expedition's exact location was in doubt but he knew they were still too far north of Monterey — perhaps as much as 200 miles. That fact did not concern the expedition leaders as much as the question of how many miles lay between them and the coast? They questioned Sylvestre but he claimed to know nothing about the lands or the people that lay west of his home near Utah Lake.

While they were camped, a hunting party killed a second bison, smaller than the big bull they had taken a few days earlier but it did provide fresh meat. While at the river camp the Laguna Indian boy, now answering to the name Joaquín, was racing across a grassy meadow on one of the expedition's best horses. The animal hit a hole with both front feet and went over on its back. Joaquín was thrown clear and landed without injury on the boggy earth. The horse was not so fortunate. It struggled to its feet but could not completely raise its head. Its neck had been injured, perhaps even broken. Joaquín wept inconsolably and had to be reassured that he would not be banished.

"According to our guide, one cannot cross anywhere else than by the single ford . . . which lies on the side west of the hogback on the north, very near to a chain of small bluffs of loose dirt."
Sept. 13. The Green River crossing.

Two days later the party moved a mile upriver to the crossing. Water came nearly up to the bottoms of the packs but the river bottom was firm. The injured horse, unable to raise its head struggled to keep its nose above water. Joaquín rode alongside, tearfully urging the creature on. A cheer went up when it finally emerged onto the west bank. The animal had spirit, there was hope it might recover. Silvestre informed the padres that the territory they now rode on was the beginning of his peoples' lands.

Chapter 4

WEST TO THE
LAGUNA PEOPLE

The Indian and bison trails that converged on the east side of the Green River began to separate on the opposite bank like strands of spider web radiating outwards towards the southwest. Silvestre urged his mount onto one of the more prominent tracks. Had they gone straight west they would have had to negotiate a high bluff. A few miles later, at the top of a ridge, Sylvestre pointed towards the country to the north. Ragged, broken hills and bluffs twisted and turned until obscured by the horizon. Sylvestre gestured towards the south.

"As soon as we reached the top we found tracks . . . about twelve horses and some people on foot . . . indications . . . they had been lying in wait or spying for some time."

Sept. 16.

More flat and hospitable yet desert-like, the terrain seemed to stretch on forever until swallowed up in the haze of distance.

Several hours later they topped another stony ridge. No one could have missed the message. Dozens of horse tracks were churned into the dry, dusty earth and among them — moccasin prints.

Captain Miera gazed off to the northeast — towards the expedition's back trail. This particular ridge had provided an excellent location to observe anyone traveling from that direction. Was it the Utes or was it Comanches who had crossed into Ute territory? Silvestre examined the tracks but gave no sign of recognition.

That night, when it came time to sleep, the Indian guide bedded down some distance from the rest of the party and wrapped himself in the bright red blanket he had been given — something he had not previously done. A night wind was blowing from the northwest, enough to muffle the sounds of anyone approaching the camp from downwind. Was Silvestre waiting for an attack by his own people? Was the red blanket a way for night raiders to keep from confusing the Laguna guide with expedition members? Yet the Laguna boy Joaquín lay blissfully sleeping in his own blankets between the two priests just as he had done every night since they had left the Ute camp on Grand Mesa. It was obvious he knew nothing. Even so, the Spaniards slept lightly, the few weapons they had, close at hand.

As soon as it was light enough to see, the men packed up and moved out. Dawn came slowly, announced by the guttural cry of a raven passing overhead. The bird flew effortlessly, almost tauntingly towards the west, and soon it was out of sight. In the half light of the new day Silvestre seemed confused, unsure of exactly which route to take and at times he rode behind the party. Muskets were kept at the ready. Numerous pairs of eyes fastened their gaze on anything that appeared to move, anything that might indicate another human presence on nearby ridges. Finally, Silvestre retook the lead and continued towards the southwest. Periodically the Spaniards crossed fresh horse tracks. It was apparent the unidentified riders were staying ahead, out of sight —

watching. That evening just before camp was made, two expedition members angled off and disappeared through the high brush intent on circling around in hopes of catching a glimpse of whoever was watching them. Their only reward was more tracks.

The following morning, September 17, Silvestre led the Spaniards directly along the fresh trail left by the mystery riders — studying and watching the horizon. Finally he muttered a single word — *Comanche*. The Laguna immediately turned his horse towards the northwest. The expedition followed. They crossed a low ridge and dropped into a dry, shallow valley. The Laguna guide headed towards a series of ascending ridges and rock benches. The ground was hard, unyielding and littered with stones, but the horses and mules left few tracks and no dust. Finally, hidden behind a narrow ridge, they stopped. The Spaniards held the high ground. Anyone who attempted to follow had to cross the open valley. Afterwards they would have to enter this same maze of serpentine formations of rock ledges — a perfect place for an ambush. Pursuers would think twice about taking the risk. Even Captain Miera was impressed with Silvestre's tactics. Suspicions against the Laguna diminished. The day wore on. The men continued to watch their back trail for signs of pursuit.

At one point, on a still higher ridge line, Silvestre paused and pointed out the junction of the Uinta and Duchesne Rivers far below. The Uinta had ceased to flow, having been reduced to a series of long, shallow ponds and puddles by the autumn dryness. The heights commanded a sweeping vista of the southern horizon, views of seventy to eighty miles, land dotted with intermittent stands of gnarled and stunted cedar trees. To the west lay a series of buff-colored buttes. The land itself was becoming more worn and eroded — eaten away by time, wind and water.

A short time later the expedition rode past the remains of a circular-shaped ruin. Broken grinding stones and shards of clay pottery littered the ground. The site had obviously not been inhabited for genera-tions, perhaps longer. Beyond the ruins Silvestre pulled his mount to a stop and pointed to the south-west — a thin wisp of smoke had climbed into the morning air. Was it a taunt from the group that had been stalking them or smoke from a hunting camp of Silvestre's own people? That did not seem

"We saw ruins . . . where there were fragments of stones for grinding maize, of jars, and of pots of clay . . . the ruins now almost completely in mounds."

Sept. 17.

likely. Why would a hunting camp deliberately advertise its presence? The Laguna said nothing but immediately led the expedition down from the heights and into the valley of the Duchesne River, working the terrain to keep the expedition and its animals out of sight. It was impossible to hide the trail of that many riders and pack animals, but once he reached the river he led them through a series of marshes. Five times that day they made a river crossing, zigzagging but always holding a westerly course. Silvestre was making it difficult for anyone who might pursue them. That fact was recognized but the men still cursed and complained as branches and brush scraped faces and snagged clothing.

Despite the uncertainties of the day and a difficult ride, Escalante wrote that night in the journal, *"There is good land along these three rivers that we crossed today and plenty of it for farming with the aid of irrigation — beautiful cottonwood groves, fine pastures, timber and firewood not too far away, for three settlements.*" Silvestre had led them across the lower Duchesne, the Lake Fork and the upper Duchesne. Their camp that night was about a mile above the future town of Duchesne, Utah.

"Irrigation ditches could be dug for watering the land on this side."
Sept. 16. West of Jensen, Utah.

The next morning Silvestre continued breaking trail where none had previously existed. A horse gashed its leg on a sharp rock and a short time later the expedition was forced to back-track nearly a mile when they could no longer force their way through the tangled river bottom vegetation. A few hours later he entered into a narrow canyon which contained thousands of swallow nests high on the rock walls. The residents of the mud nests had already left for the season. The only sounds were those of hooves picking through the loose rocks underfoot. The narrow gorge was a perfect place for an ambush, but none came. The rock walls opened again and the riders entered a level plain where they crossed a well-traveled north-south trail. Silvestre ignored it, intent on holding a westerly heading.

All that day a cold wind blew down from the Uinta Mountains to the north, their crests dusted with the first snows of a coming winter. It was a reminder that September was nearly gone and no one had brought winter clothing. It was an issue that had never even been discussed, so sure were they that by this time they would have crossed into California. Instead, the expedition was somewhere in a wilderness, two or three hundred miles north of Monterey with no idea how far west they still had to travel. Riders hunched beneath their woolen ponchos, legs tucked close to the warm flesh of their horses.

The land was growing increasingly rugged. The hills were higher, the canyons deeper and the vegetation was becoming more forest-like with isolated stands of aspen and pine. The dried bison meat was nearly gone. Flour for bread and cornmeal for tortillas were disappearing faster than anyone wanted to admit. On the positive side there was plenty of water and the horses and mules did not lack for grass.

During the hours of darkness the cold mountain wind died and so did the injured horse. The animal had managed to

"There is good land . . . that we crossed today . . . beautiful popular groves, fine pastures, timber and firewood.

Sept. 18. West of Jensen.

keep up with the expedition through six days of difficult marches, sometimes lagging behind but always managing to catch up. Unable to eat properly, the creature had lost considerable flesh. Its endurance had reached the end. Now it lay in the grass where it had made its final bed — flat on the ground as if in a deep sleep. The men saddled, packed and rode away. They could not help thinking this might be an omen of things to come.

By mid-day the land flattened slightly and sagebrush began to appear, intermixed with more and more stands of trees. Reduced visibility sometimes made it difficult to see more than a few yards ahead. It would be a bad place to meet an enemy. Muskets were kept primed and ready. A dozen pairs of eyes peered ahead into the forest gloom. Ears strained to catch any unusual sounds. The mules were watched for abnormal signs of behavior. They would likely be the first to know if something was amiss. Silvestre gradually swung towards the southwest again, climbing a long incline, then west again for nearly eight miles across a sagebrush flat interspersed with prickly pear cactus. It was terrain comparable to a New Mexico landscape but a freshening wind from the north was a chilly reminder that home lay far to the southeast. Escalante wrote the following morning, *"Last night it was so cold that even the water which stood close to the fire all night was frozen by morning. Today 24 miles."*

The party rode through what is now Strawberry Reservoir traversing another region of sagebrush flats then back through more wooded ridges. Silvestre seemed impatient, urging his mount on and several times he disappeared ahead of the riders. Exasperated, Domínguez ordered the guide to slow down and stay in sight. At the top of a high promontory the Laguna finally paused and pointed westward. He could see the hills of his homeland. The riders worked their way down the ridge through stands of chokecherry, scrub oak and aspen so thick they wondered if the packs would stay on the mules. Again Silvestre went ahead almost out of sight. Domínguez rode after him. In doing so he caught his knee between his horse's flank and an aspen tree, bruising it badly. When he finally caught up with the guide he indicated, with no uncertainty, that the Laguna was not to stray from his sight. Together they rode to the bottom of the ridge and there the excited guide pointed to a small stream.

"Then we went down to medium-sized river in which good trout breed in abundance, two of which Joaquín the Laguna killed with arrows."

Sept. 21.

It was flowing west. They had crossed the divide and were on their way down into Utah Valley. The priest could better understand the guide's hurry. Silvestre was almost home.

After a strenuous descent the expedition camped in a meadow of tall grass. The wind continued to blow almost until dawn. Escalante wrote in the journal that night, *"Today 17 miles. Tonight we felt the cold more than in the previous ones."*

Little time was wasted the next morning packing and moving out. Silvestre had informed the group that today they would make contact with his people. Late in the afternoon the expedition crested another ridge and they paused. Far ahead lay the waters of Utah Lake. Some distance east of the shining waters several columns of smoke floated lazily upwards — signal fires, Silvestre said. The Spaniards had been spotted. The guide lit his own fire and piled on green fir branches until his own cloud of white smoke drifted upwards into the azure sky. A short time later more fires were observed in the valley ahead. Camp was made on a ridge, and in the belief that some of his people might reach the expedition an hour or two after midnight, Silvestre kept watch. He periodically called out that it was a peaceful party sleeping nearby, but the dark, shadowed woods below him remained silent. Nor were there any columns of smoke in the sky the next morning.

Escalante and his companions were about to meet a new people and what better day than this? It was September 23, feast day for Our Lady of Mercy — Mary, mother of Christ. He wrote, *"This coincidence seemed like a happy omen of the good disposition of these captives, whose liberty we desired and besought of the Redeemer of the world through His immaculate Mother's intercession . . . ."*

Domínguez opened a pack of trade goods and gave Silvestre and Joaquín each a yard of brightly colored woolen cloth and an equal length of scarlet ribbon. The two Lagunas secured their gifts around their heads allowing the ends to trail down their backs. Silvestre wrapped himself in his red blanket and proudly led the band of riders down the hillside towards the waters of the largest lake any of them had ever seen. Twice, on the way down, they passed hot sulfurous springs similar to those in New Mexico.

"Some men came out . . . with weapons in hand to defend their homes and families . . . Silvestre spoke to them."

Sept. 23.

Ahead of them smoke appeared, but this time in great swirling clouds. Silvestre scowled. Something was wrong. Emerging from the trees they saw Laguna warriors setting fire to the meadow that lay between themselves and the approaching Spaniards. After the rest of the expedition had reined to a halt, Domínguez, Silvestre, Joaquín and Andrés galloped ahead, staying clear of the spreading flames. They approached a line of warriors on foot, equipped for battle. Silvestre called out, his voice audible above the crackle of burning grass. Weapons were lowered. Minutes later he was joyously embracing old friends. The four riders, surrounded by a babble of excited voices, were escorted to a nearby village. The remainder of the expedition moved up-wind from the grass fire, now almost burned out, and made camp.

A short time later, to an assembled crowd, Silvestre recounted the journey from Grand Mesa to Utah Lake. He told how well he and Joaquín had been treated. He talked at length about the bravery of the Spaniards who had unflinchingly ridden into Comanche country relying on only their God to protect them. He recalled the uncertain days beyond the Green River, and the mysterious stalkers who never showed themselves — held back, he believed, by the God of the priest at whose side he now stood. No one could have provided a better introduction for the New Mexico wanderers. Not to be left out, the boy, Joaquín, " . . . *haughtily proud* . . . " announced that he intended to stay with the expedition and did not leave Domínguez' side except to care for the padre's horse.

Meanwhile more lake dwellers appeared from other villages and Silvestre's story was told and retold. Finally, after a great crowd had assembled, Domínguez, using Silvestre and Andrés as interpreters, began to preach. Unlike the unresponsive group to which he had spoken on Grand Mesa a month earlier, the Laguna people listened eagerly.

At the end of his sermon he told them that should they choose to accept the teachings of " . . . *a single true God, to love Him and obey Him* . . . ," Domínguez and his brother, Escalante, would return, bringing other priests to teach and baptize. Teachers would instruct the Lagunas in farming, the raising of livestock and the making of cloth. Soldiers would come to stand between the Lagunas and their enemies. His talk was received with enthusiasm. A large fire burned all that night as Silvestre, in his newly assumed role as ambassador to Spain and the Church, told his listeners, " . . . *the padres spoke the truth, that in their company one could travel all over the earth without risk, and that they were nothing but good people."*

The next morning Domínguez remained alone in the village while his companions brought in the rest of the expedition. When it arrived the men were greeted by an even larger crowd than had gathered the previous afternoon. Once again, Domínguez preached, this time assisted by Escalante. Afterwards the chiefs and elders held council with the two preachers. They had considered their words, " . . . *and all unanimously replied that the padres should come . . . and that they offered all their land to the Spaniards for them to build their homes wherever they pleased."*

The chiefs would also welcome Spanish soldiers to help resist outside intruders who raided the valley, killing and plundering. Domínguez asked for a token that he might take back to the Spanish king attesting to the Laguna's sincerity. It was promised. In return, the expedition gave out gifts. In less than a heartbeat the leading chiefs went from the age of stone to that of iron. Steel bladed butcher knives were held aloft as though they were treasures from heaven itself. Domínguez later wrote, "*To all the other*

"We presented the chief . . . with a big all-purpose knife and white glass beads. To all the other individuals we gave white beads, a few to each one since they were so many."

Sept. 24.

individuals we gave white beads, a few to each one since they were many, and for which they were very happy and grateful."

The excitement finally ebbed and the expedition leaders found opportunity to converse with the chiefs and elders of several villages. Domínguez explained the need for a new guide since Silvestre had told them he had no knowledge about the country which lay beyond Utah Lake, and had no desire to travel further. The chiefs made clear none of their people knew the way to the coast but agreed to provide a warrior fluent in some of the languages the expedition would encounter. The offer was accepted and the new guide was christened José María. He was presented with identical gifts as those given to Silvestre on Grand Mesa.

Two other requests had been made of the Laguna people. Joachín, who had no close family, wanted to continue with the expedition, and the Spaniards needed supplies. It was agreed that the Laguna boy could continue on and return the following year with Domínguez and Escalante. As for the concern about food, the Lagunas were willing to supply the padres with enough dried fish to fill their nearly empty panniers. The generous gesture would provide food for perhaps three weeks and help stretch out the remaining stores of flour and cornmeal.

Three days after their meeting the Lagunas, the expedition was packed and ready for the trail once more. The gift to the king of Spain was ready, a finely

"All bade us farewell most tenderly, especially Silvestre, who hugged us tightly, practically in tears. They expected us back within a year."

Sept. 25.

tanned deer skin upon which had been painted four figures representing four leading Laguna chiefs. In each of the four corners was a small red cross, copied from one they had seen on a rosary carried by an expedition member. Domínguez, overcome with emotion, told the people present should illness or enemies attack them before the priests could return, they were to call out, "*God, the true One, help us, protect us.*" Hearing they could not properly form the words in Spanish he changed the prayer to, "*Jesus-Mary, Jesus-Mary.*" The words soon became a chant caught up by the entire group of Lagunas. Silvestre rode a short ways with the party before saying a final good-bye, and the last sounds the expedition heard coming from the Laguna gathering were those of, "*Jesús-María, Jesús-María.*"

The valley leading to the south was impressive, and where Provo now stands Escalante wrote it would be possible to build "*two or even three good settlements.*" He believed the Utah Valley could support the entire population of New Mexico, with land left over. Captain Miera was even more enthusiastic. He had been told that north of the lake lay still more land, rich and fertile. He estimated that Utah Lake was nearly 16 miles wide and 40 long. (Its actual measurements are closer to 13 wide and 25 miles long.) Its waters were rich with fish. The land surrounding it provided cottontail and jack rabbits with a variety of wild game birds.

Miera had also been told there were bison to the north — great herds of the shaggy beasts. He wished he could have made a two day ride in that direction to another lake said to be many times larger than Utah Lake and so salty fish could not live beneath its waters. Miera could not shake the hope that this lake might actually be an inland extension of the Pacific Ocean. He intended to find out when they returned the following year but, for now, there was the urgency to press on towards Monterey. To do that the expedition had to pick up a southwesterly heading. Time was important. Winter was not far away.

The Spaniards had not gotten away from the Laguna camp until early in the afternoon, so their march was short. That night they camped near present day Springville, Utah.

The following afternoon the expedition's new guide, José María, and Joachín, scouting the way ahead, returned with five non-Lagunas who were fed and given a small gift of tobacco. The visitors proved as amiable and friendly as their neighbors to the north. They stayed and visited until nearly midnight but nothing was learned about a trail that would lead west.

September 28 was unusually warm, and again José María, Joachín, and Andrés had gone on ahead to search for more Indians. The expedition was riding through a grove of cottonwoods, when " . . . *eight Indians approached us with great fear, most of them naked with only a piece of buckskin over the private parts.*" With no interpreters present the priests made repeated efforts to communicate but were unsuccessful. After a short time the strangers melted back into the willows. It had been a contact from which no one profited.

The following day a similar scene occurred but this time the interpreters were present. Domínguez explained the gospel, and the six new listeners were attentive and expressed their pleasure that the padres planned to return the following summer. These, too, knew nothing about what lay to the west.

A short time later the expedition discovered a hut inhabited by a very old man with " . . . *a beard so full and long that he looked like one of the ancient hermits of Europe*" wrote Escalante. Miera was impressed enough to sketch the withered old face while the bearded one was questioned by José María. The old man indicated he knew of nothing good that lay to the west. He believed the expedition should continue southwest, but where that would lead them, he did not know.

That evening the expedition camped on the grassy banks of the Sevier River a few miles south of the present town of Nephi. Captain Miera took a latitude reading. They were still 100 miles north of a due west bearing for Monterey. In a few more days they would need to turn west but the old man had warned them if they went that way they would encounter high mountains, deserts and little water. This sounded similar to descriptions given of terrain a few dozen miles inland from the coast. Were these observations and those given by the old man descriptions of the same land? Miera was becoming more convinced that California could not be that much further — a week of travel at most. He vigorously imparted his opinion to both Domínguez and Escalante. He was somewhat satisfied the next morning when the valley did begin to open up and the expedition was able to turn more westerly to avoid a line of high hills directly in their path. Travel became easier as the men rode through thin groves of gnarled piñon trees. After crossing a series of ridges, the terrain flattened out. Isolated patches of salt flats could be seen glistening in the afternoon sun. Finding water might prove difficult but the flat, open country beckoned them on. Miera watched carefully for a gap in the high rolling hills to the west.

At day-break, only a short time after the men had turned out of their blankets, twenty strangers walked boldly into camp. A greeting was extended to José María. These were rabbit hunters. Each man carried a club, a bow, a quiver of arrows and a long, narrow yucca fiber net. Each individual was fully bearded, wore a small piece of polished bone through the lower cartilage of his nose, and was wrapped in a blanket woven from narrow strips of furry rabbit skin. The strangers demonstrated how several nets could be strung together between bushes forming a long barrier. Rabbits could be driven into the nets and dispatched with an arrow or a club. For proof one hunter held up a dead jackrabbit he had killed a short time earlier.

It was an amiable group and Captain Miera recalled stories by Indian visitors to Santa Fe who told of bearded hunters in the interior regions who looked very much like Spaniards. He made sketches of several individuals and their gear to include in his own report. When questioned about what lay to the west, the visitors could only shrug.

The last warm days of September were over. The mornings held a hint of winter. The land had become more desert-like and nowhere through the ridges to the west could anyone see evidence of a trail that might lead to California.

Chapter 5

⚔ THE DECISION ⚔

T he first day of October, 1776, found the expedition entering increasingly dry country. The men rode through miles of twisted, stunted sagebrush that had been imprisoned in wind-drifted sand. An increasingly rugged wall of hills met the sky on the western horizon — terrain that appeared to be too difficult to climb with horses and mules. The Spaniards continued their southwesterly heading. Of more concern was the lack of water. Riders fanned out across the plain, some to the west, others to the east, but they found nothing. The land remained flat and empty except for the ubiquitous and wind-tortured clumps of sagebrush.

In the early afternoon they saw what appeared to be a lake far ahead. Thirteen miles later they realized what they had been riding towards had been nothing more than a dry alkaline basin. They covered 36 miles that day and the horses and mules were exhausted and thirsty.

After camp had been made, five scouts were sent further ahead to search for water. If they found it, one man would return to guide the rest of the party on. It was a bright moon-lit night and for several hours those who had been left behind waited, but no one returned. Two guards were posted to watch the thirsty animals then everyone else fell into an exhausted sleep.

"Ahead . . . lay a wide plain without any pasturage or water source whatsoever.

Oct. 5. South of Delta.

Morning came. The horses and mules were gone. The guards had surrendered to their own weariness. Only Cisneros had taken the precaution of keeping his mount tied near him during the night. Angrily, without even taking time to saddle, he mounted bareback and began following the tracks of the herd back to the northeast. He knew they would lead toward the last muddy pool the animals had stopped at. The herd had almost drank it dry. There would not be enough water for a second visit. Cisneros rode hard and made contact with the stray animals a few miles from camp. They had obviously left camp not long before dawn. He turned the herd around. The sun had almost reached its zenith when the lone rider and his charges reached the camp again. The five scouts sent out the night before still had not returned.

"The chief was already advanced in years, yet not aged, and of very good appearance. They stayed talking very happily with us, and in the briefest time won our great affection."

Oct. 2.

An hour after Cisneros had brought the horse herd in, four of the missing men rode into camp accompanied by five bearded Indians on foot. They were friendly and aware of the situation the Spaniards were facing. In the sandy earth they sketched out the route which would lead to the nearest water — about a three hour ride towards the hills to the west.

Afterwards four of the Indians left to search for the missing scout. They found him sometime later, making his way back to camp — having been no more successful than his companions at finding water.

While the horses were being saddled and packs loaded, Domínguez and Escalante gave a short teaching sermon to this latest group of Indians. It was a halting effort, given first to Andrés in Spanish so that he could translate it into Ute after which José María, the Laguna Ute, converted it into a mixture of Ute words and sign language. The listeners, having been joined by several other companions who had wondered in, listened expectantly.

Escalante wrote that evening: *"We took our leave of them, and all, the chief especially, kept holding us by the hand with great tenderness and affection. But where they expressed themselves the most was when we were already leaving this place. Scarcely did they see us depart when all — burst out crying . . . we kept hearing the tender laments of these unfortunate little sheep of Christ, lost along the way simply for not having the Light. They touched our hearts so much that some of our companions could not hold back the tears."*

Less than three hours later the expedition found water where they had been told. It was tainted with alkali but drinkable and nearby was enough forage to keep the herd from straying. There was no need to post guards that night.

October 3 was another day of detours around and through what had become a growing number of marshes in the vicinity of what is now Clear Lake, south of Delta, Utah. At one point Andrés' horse fell and the guide was pitched head-first into the slimy muck. His face was bruised and perhaps his ego, but he remounted and rode on, wiping the stinging alkali mud from his eyes. Earlier in the trip the incident might have been treated with merriment but not now. That night they camped near an alkali-laced pool where every man and animal was able to satisfy a growing thirst. There was also abundant grass — the first the animals had in three days. For the men it was a different story. The flour and cornmeal were nearly gone, and the dried fish they had brought from Utah Lake was edible but it was a diet only José María and Joachín were able to accept without complaint. They had lived their lives eating the almost flavorless flesh interlaced with bones. The men wished that a bison, even a tough, stringy bull would appear.

Conversation had increasingly turned towards memorable meals and special dishes prepared by distant mothers, aunts and wives. Although such talk helped to pass the hours, it did nothing to alleviate the problem of hunger. The men kept their muskets primed and ready, but no game appeared. Even the rabbits were gone.

A new problem presented itself the next morning. Two days of alkali water was having a cathartic effect on the men as well as the horses and mules. The forage the animals had consumed emerged from their bodies as streams of green, half-digested liquid. To make things more trying, a cold south wind had been blowing for two days. At times gusts were strong enough to repattern the swirls in the sand beneath the clumps of never-ending sage. Each man hunched down in his saddle, poncho wrapped tightly, neck scarf covering his face and eyes which had to be held nearly shut to protect them from the stinging wind and sand.

That evening in camp Cisneros, seldom one for diplomacy even under the best of conditions, spoke sharply to his servant, Simón Lucero. An instant later the master was on his

"It was already dark when they returned saying that they had not found any pass . . . for getting to Monterey . . . we decided to continue south."

Oct. 5.

back in the sand shielding himself from blows to his head. Lucero was pulled off and the two men held apart until their tempers cooled. In New Mexico Cisneros would never have been questioned by Lucero much less physically assaulted, but in this desert and under these conditions social standing had almost lost its meaning. Thirst, hunger, frustration and the never-ending days in the saddle were beginning to strip away the veneer of civilization. Cisneros received neither support nor sympathy from his companions. The incident was dropped although Joachín, never having seen a fight between Spaniards was badly frightened. He refused to leave the sides of the two priests for the remainder of that night. José María, the Laguna guide, also was deeply affected. He made his bed a considerable distance away from the camp, then at dawn, slipped away on foot and headed north towards his own people. *"We saw him leave,"* wrote Escalante, *"but did not want to say anything to him, nor to have him followed and brought back . . . ."*

The men were silent that morning and the wind had stopped. In early afternoon it regained its strength, and brought from the north dark, sullen clouds and dropping temperatures. Snow began to fall, lightly at first, but by the time camp was made that evening several inches of heavy, wet slush covered the ground. It was impossible to build fires.

Each man awoke the next morning buried in wet snow. Visibility was down to a few yards. Expedition members joined together in twos and threes, hidden beneath their blankets waiting for the snow to stop. Hours passed. Throughout the day heavy, wet flakes continued to fall. Horses and mules stood pressed together, tails to the wind. Snow melted from their backs and trickled down their bodies only to freeze again on bellies and legs.

"Today we suffered greatly from the cold . . . .Winter had already set in most severely, for all the sierras . . . in all directions were covered with snow."

Oct. 8.

The half light of day finally faded into the blackest of nights. The entire group was now huddled together beneath a make-shift tent of blankets. Pannier covers had been laid on the snow and over them were placed saddle blankets. It helped to insulate from the snow beneath and kept at least part of the wetness from soaking through the mens' clothing. The snow continued.

The two priests led their followers in prayer. Escalante wrote, *" . . . we implored the intercession of Our Mother and Patroness by praying aloud in common the three parts of her rosary and by chanting the Litany, the one of All-Saints. And God was pleased that by nine at night it ceased to snow . . . "*

Daylight came. The snow was too deep and wet for travel, and with no dry firewood, there was no way to warm up. To make matters worse the wind returned — again from the frigid north. The expedition spent another miserable day and night huddled together in the snow.

By the dawn of October 8, the snow had settled enough to allow travel. Stiff fingers loaded wet packs and pulled saddle girths tight. The ground beneath was soft and miry. Mud balled up beneath the animal's hooves. Periodically one would stumble and fall. Nine exhausting miles later the day ended and another fireless camp was made.

That night, beneath their still-wet blankets, Domínguez and Escalante talked quietly, out of earshot of everyone but the ever present Joachín. All that day the two expedition leaders had looked towards the hills in the west. As deep as the snow was in the valley, what would it be like in the high country? Moral was the lowest it had been since they had left Santa Fe. They were down to little more than a week's supply of dry fish and a small quantity of corn. It was time to make a decision. If they turned west towards California, who would guide them through the passes? They could easily die — trapped by deepening snows. The priests looked at Joachín. They could not risk the life of the Indian boy, nor those of their other companions. Furthermore, if a mountain crossing was successful and the expedition reached Monterey, they could not return to Santa Fe until the following June at the earliest. That would make it impossible to return to the Laguna Utes by early summer as they had promised.

After weighing all the options a decision was reached, *". . . we thereupon decided to continue south . . . as far as the El Río Colorado, and from here point our way towards Cosnina,*

Moqui, and Zuñi." From Zuñi it would be an easy journey on to Santa Fe. The following year, using the Laguna camps at Utah Lake as a base, they could complete the journey to the coast, hopefully better equipped, earlier in the season and during more favorable weather.

The next morning Domínguez called the expedition members together and informed them of the decision that he and Escalante had made the night before. No one spoke except Captain Miera. He met the announcement with protest and exclaimed that they were directly east of Monterey. Surely California could be no more than a week away. The captain was emphatic! They had come too far and had risked too much to accept defeat now. Domínguez silenced him with a raised hand.

"Don Bernardo had been saying . . . we could reach Monterey . . . within a week."

Oct. 12.

The decision had been made. They would return to Santa Fe.

For three days the riders trailed south. The sun returned and soon there were pools of water standing everywhere, sweet and fresh. Forage, most of which lay beneath the snow, was scarce but by snatching at clumps of grass when they appeared, the animals could survive. Miera, on the other hand, had begun to exhibit a coldness towards the two priests. The attitude was soon picked up by other expedition members, especially Laín and the interpreter, Andrés. Escalante wrote, " . . . *They came along very peevishly . . . all unbearably irksome. Their conversations had no other topic than the negative results they would derive from such a lengthy trip."* Escalante restated the arguments advanced by Domínguez, *"But they listened to none of this . . .* " Captain Miera convinced nearly everyone that there would be, " *. . . honors and profit from . . . reaching Monterey and . . . now he was assuring them that we had deprived them of these blessings . . .* " By October 11, the priests were isolated from all but Joachín.

The group was approaching a high ridge directly in their line of march, and to the west, perhaps a day's ride away, appeared a gap in the previously impenetrable wall of hills. It stood like a beacon on the horizon.

The two leaders rode out of camp that morning behind everyone else and remaining out of earshot — they talked. They were convinced that a revolt was in the making and they had to end it. " *. . . We decided to lay aside the . . . arguments mentioned and to search anew God's will by casting lots — putting Monterey on one and Cosnina on the other — and to follow the route which came out.* " The two rejoined their

"We . . . halted fearing that further on we would not find water for tonight."

Oct. 10. A day north of where lots were cast.

companions and Domínguez ordered a halt. Everyone gathered around him. He began to speak.

If God had meant for them to reach Monterey, why had they not done so by now? Why had so many obstacles been placed in their path? Was it right, in God's eyes, to risk the lives of anyone, especially the boy Joachín, for financial gain? There was silence. Eyes began to shift away from the steady gaze of the priest. Even Miera twisted uncomfortably in his saddle. Domínguez presented the solution he and Escalante had agreed upon. He then commanded each man to dismount, drop to his knees and ask for God's guidance in this matter, and to accept the outcome " . . . *in a Christian spirit . . . .*"

It is not recorded if sticks or slips of paper were used but " . . . *the one of Cosnina came out. This we all heartily accepted now, thanks be to God . . .* " The riders gave one last look

"We decided to . . . search anew God's will by casting lots—putting Monterey on one and Cosnina on the other . . . ."
Oct. 11. Detail from an outdoor mural in Paonia, CO.
by Ginny Allen.

towards the gap in the hills to the west, and then began to climb through the ridge that lay in their path. By late afternoon it was behind them. They were headed home. The land flattened out and that night they camped in a valley north of present day Cedar City, Utah. Fertile earth had replaced sand. Grass was plentiful and the sea of sagebrush they had ridden through for so many days was now behind them. There was no more talk of California.

A day later the expedition surprised some twenty Indian women collecting seeds. All fled but two who were left, frozen by fear. "It pained us to see them frightened so much that they could not even speak, and we tried to take away their fear and misgivings through the interpreter and Joaquín, the Laguna. These Indian women were so poorly dressed that they wore only some pieces of deerskin hanging from the waist, barely covering what one cannot gaze upon without peril."

With a mixture of Ute and sign language the boy, Joaquín, eventually eased the womens' fears and reassured them that no harm would come. He asked what lay to the south and to the southeast. The answers came haltingly. The women talked of a great river beyond which lived people who dressed in red and blue cloth. Escalante knew that both red and blue cloth from Santa Fe was regularly traded to Indians living to the northwest of his mission station at Zuñi. Perhaps they were closer to home than they thought. In a final effort, young Joaquín tried to impress upon the women that the Spaniards had come in peace and asked them to inform the men of their band that further talks would be desirable. The pair of seed gatherers slipped away through the brush.

Two hours later the riders again surprised a small group of native people, this time men. They all fled but Laín spurred his horse into pursuit and at a gallop, leaned down from his mount, easily sweeping one runner up into the saddle. With his kicking and squirming charge held firmly in his free arm he returned to the expedition. *"The Indian . . . was so intimidated that he appeared to be out of his mind,"* penned Escalante.

The captive calmed down and was given food. A brightly colored ribbon was attached to his hair — already adorned with two narrow strips of red and blue cloth. He carried no weapons, only a long net made from strands of twisted yucca fiber — a rabbit hunter.

Escalante wanted to know where he had acquired the red and blue cloth. The man could not or would not say — only that they had come from a trade he had made the previous summer. He did speak at length about the Colorado River. In almost every way his story matched that of the women but when asked if he had ever heard of bearded men living east of where the red and blue cloth came from he *" . . . answered that there weren't any . . . "*

The Indian was handed a kernel of corn and asked if he knew where more might be obtained. Recognition flickered in his eyes but despite repeated questioning, he gave only a confusing account of people living on one side of a river next to another small river. His words had no meaning. Finally, tempted with more food, he agreed to spend the night.

They broke camp the next morning, packed and fell in behind the rabbit hunter. He had been promised a steel knife if he would guide the expedition to a crossing point at the Colorado River. A few hours later he led them into a small temporary encampment containing one hunter near his own age, a very old man, three women and several children. It was only then the guide brought out a small bag of corn to show Escalante. It was obvious it was something he valued highly. He also exhibited what appeared to be the family's entire food supply. In addition to the bag of the corn there were a few small woven containers of piñon nuts and a quantity of dried yucca pods. The group had so little the Spaniards did not ask if they could exchange provisions for trade goods. Through sign language the three males of the camp were told that if any one of them would help lead the Spaniards to the river they too would be given steel knives and glass beads.

The old man lovingly ran his thumb along the edge of a shiny blade. He would go, he said, he and the rabbit hunter who had led the expedition into camp. As they had done in each case previously, the knives were then presented. The old one spoke to his companions and they began to break camp. Afterwards as he and the rabbit hunter took the lead, the remaining members of his family disappeared into the bluffs carrying their few possessions.

The expedition continued south until mid-afternoon. The old man and his companion led the riders through a winding, twisting rock labyrinth. Shielded from sight for a moment, the two slipped through a gap in the rocks and were gone. There was no way anyone on horseback could follow. The clever old man had seen to it that his family was safely away, and now, new knives in hand, he and his younger companion had cleverly engineered their own escape. Even though the ruse cost valuable time backtracking, Escalante wrote, "*We applauded their cleverness in having brought us through a place so well suited for carrying out their ruse . . .* "

The remainder of the day was spent threading through similar terrain. There was adequate grass, water and firewood that night as expedition members made camp within what are now the city limits of Toquerville, Utah. Escalante penned into his journal that evening these words, " *. . . today, the river cottonwoods were so green and leafy, the flowers and bloom which the land produces so flamboyant and without damage whatsoever, that they indicated there had been no freezing or frosting around here. Today 10 miles.*"

Continuing south the next morning, the expedition found a platform raised high off the ground which contained ears of corn, still in the shuck. Corn stalks had been piled over the ears to protect them from birds. Not far away were three small fields from which the grain had been harvested. Well-constructed irrigation ditches obviously had been used to bring water from nearby Ash Creek. Despite a careful search, no one could find any evidence that the owners were

"Here we found a well-constructed primitive arbor with plenty of ears and shocks of corn which had been placed on top."

Oct. 15.

nearby. The Spaniards continued on, leaving the storage platform undisturbed. Later, near the present site of Hurricane, Utah, they rode across several sets of human tracks but never caught so much as a glimpse of the people who made them. That night they camped in a deep gully which contained both a water hole and forage for the animals. They made tortillas with the last of their cornmeal. All were convinced that having found the supply of corn that morning, they would make contact with local Indians sometime the following day and be able to replenish their own supplies through trade. Escalante wrote, *"Tonight our provisions ran out completely, with nothing left but two little slabs of chocolate for tomorrow."*

October 16 found the expedition on a continuing southerly course. Mid-morning they saw eight Indians peering down at them from a steep bluff. After a great deal of pleading and gesturing on the part of the interpreter, Andrés, the eight made their way cautiously down the steep face. Once among the Spaniards the visitors made signs that

" . . . *we got onto good open country and crossed a brief plain.*"
Oct. 15. Just inside the Arizona border.

they wanted to trade. Each Indian had a quantity of
turquoise, drilled and strung on yucca fiber strings as well as
a number of small sea shells Escalante knew could only have
come from the ocean. Despite attempts by both Andrés and
Joachín, efforts to open a meaningful dialogue proved fruit-
less. These were traveling traders who knew little about
local language or where or how local food supplies might be
obtained. They carried very little food themselves. The
traders were asked if they had seen or heard of Father
Garcés but they had not. The Spaniards suggested that if
the eight would accompany the expedition, perhaps they
might lead it to someone with corn or other provisions. The
expedition also needed guides to the Colorado River. There
would be payment. After three hours of haggling a deal was
struck. The Indians would lead the expedition to a river
crossing on the Colorado in exchange for two steel knives
and a pair of empty rawhide panniers.

The pathway the new guides picked proved incredibly difficult. In the words of Escalante, *"We came to a narrow defile so bad that it took us more than half an hour to get only three saddle mounts through. This was followed by a cliff-filled incline so ruggedly steep that even climbing it on foot would be most difficult."* It was here that the eight Indian traders, holding tightly to their new knives and the two panniers, fled upwards through the black volcanic boulders of Hurricane Cliffs.

Disgusted riders spent several hours backtracking out of the canyon into which they had been led. Twice they had been betrayed. This time no one could find any humor in the situation. The entire day had netted only three miles of meaningful travel. That night, exhausted, dispirited and unable to find water, they killed a horse, roasted a quantity of the still warm meat over a fire and boned out the remainder to cool in the night air. Captain Miera turned down his portion of the saltless and stringy meal. The stomach problem he had suffered two months previously had reappeared. For the rest, the ache in their bellies was gone temporarily, and they rolled into their blankets for an exhausted sleep.

Water was found the following morning and a short time later several of the expedition members found and picked a small quantity of edible greens they found growing in a ravine — just enough to provide everyone with a small portion that evening. By late afternoon it was obvious Miera was in trouble. The captain, doubled over with severe stomach pains and weak from hunger, could barely keep his saddle.

A halt was called for the day and a search was made through the empty food panniers. Someone had hidden several small pieces of dried squash in one — believed to have been secretly traded the previous day from one or more of the eight unfaithful Indian guides. Further searching uncovered a small lump of hard sugar, so grimy and trail-worn that it was

"Today, in so painful a day's march, we only advanced two miles south."

Oct. 16.

almost unrecognizable. A fire was started, the squash, the greens found that morning, and the lump of sugar were put into a pot to cook. The result was a thin, slightly sweet flavored broth of which the larger portion was given to the ailing captain. Everyone else shared a few sips of what remained, drained the water cask and filled their bellies with another meal of roasted horse meat.

The animals were beginning to suffer from thirst so after the meal two scouts were sent to search for water. Several other expedition members climbed a nearby mesa to visually search for a possible opening east through the cliffs. So far there had been only the blind canyon the eight traitors had led them into. They returned at dark, too optimistic in what they claimed to have observed for Escalante's satisfaction. *" . . . They could not have seen so much in so short a time . . . "* Although a beacon fire was kept burning through part of the night, the two original scouts did not return.

October 18 dawned and the group was still short two members. The good news was Miera had improved enough to ride. Packs were loaded, horses saddled and again the riders continued south, hoping to make contact with their missing companions. Near midday they were approached by five more Indians. Only one ventured within hailing range. He carried a bow and a handful of arrows. This time Domínguez and Escalante went to meet him. Carefully and slowly they climbed the bluff where the man waited. They did not know if he would defend himself or flee, but curiosity finally won out. Domínguez embraced the man, then he and Escalante seated themselves on the rock, and motioned for their new companion to do the same. Only then did Domínguez call down for Andrés and Joachín to join them. Simultaneously the Indian's companions also cautiously approached. Could the five lead the expedition to water?

By late afternoon the men and animals were quenching their thirst at two hidden rain water pools. Only three of the Indians had been willing to accompany the Spaniards, probably because they recognized that Joaquín was a Ute from the north country. These were Paiute people with a similar language. They questioned Joachín, intent on learning all they could about these bearded strangers. Finally, their suspicion ebbed and realizing these men they feared were lost and without food, they offered to trade provisions for a few yards of cloth. Joachín was to accompany them to a nearby encampment. He would take a mule with empty panniers and the cloth which would be exchanged for food.

Domínguez feared it might be a trap and was persuaded only by the confidence exhibited by the Laguna boy, that these men would keep their word. The priest finally relented but only when it was agreed one of the expedition members would accompany the young Laguna. The Paiutes chose Juan Domingo, the Pueblo Indian from south of Santa Fe. Soon two riders, leading a pack mule, disappeared into the gathering darkness behind three Indian guides whose only proven virtue, to that point, had been to lead the men to water. Prayers were said and a beacon fire was lit. Somewhere, out in the darkness, was nearly a third of the expedition members, their situations known only to themselves and God.

At ten o'clock one of the missing scouts and his horse appeared, guided by the fire. Two more hours drifted by and then came the sounds of Joachín's voice as well as those of Juan

Domingo, and the last missing scout who had been reunited with the two at the Paiute camp. It was a joyous midnight reunion. The panniers contained wild sheep meat, dried cactus pears processed into cakes and a quantity of wild plant seeds that could be cooked with the meat and the cactus. Best of all, Joachín explained, after sunup more food would be brought in for trade.

While the morning meal was still on the fire, twenty Indians approached the camp with additional quantities of cactus pear cakes and buckskin bags containing a variety of wild seeds. Trade packs were opened and deals were struck. The strings of white beads were particularly popular. Domínguez made it clear that they would trade for still more food, especially meat, piñon nuts and cactus pear cakes. The traders agreed to meet the expedition at midday with the desired items and then departed camp. A short time later, a good meal under their belts, the expedition members made minor repairs on their equipment and waited. It was October 19, and somewhere ahead lay the Colorado River.

Noon brought a new group of Paiute traders but they carried no meat, only small sacks of seeds and cactus pear cakes as well as a quantity of cactus pears that had been stripped of their needles and dried in the sun. The Paiute people, existed on seeds, the plentiful cactus fruit, rabbits and wild desert sheep. The trades that day netted a bushel of mixed seeds, and double that quantity of cactus fruits and a few piñon nuts. It was enough to provide rations for the next several days.

Escalante questioned the seed traders about Garcés, the priest/explorer who had sent the letter to Zuñi the previous summer. No one had seen or even heard of the man or his Indian companion. Questions were asked about finding a river crossing, but answers were conflicting and despite pleas for a guide, not one of the Paiutes indicated a willingness to accompany the expedition to a crossing.

With the traders that day had come a man said to be a Mescalero Apache from the country across the Colorado. He seemed to want nothing to do with the Spaniards. Escalante, wrote, *"He . . . differed from these Indians in his dislike of seeing us around here and, as we noticed, in great animosity which he purposely displayed."*

Santa Fe seemed a long way away that night to the young priest, especially after he learned Captain Miera's stomach pains had returned.

Next morning, on the advice from the Paiute traders, the expedition turned its horses towards the northeast where they had been told they would find the only safe crossing of the Colorado. Captain Miera, still suffering severe stomach cramps, hunched down in his saddle and took his usual place in the column. Later that morning they halted so that he could take a latitude reading. The effort indicated that the expedition was still 100 miles north of a direct

"Lorenzo de Olivares, driven by thirst . . . went off as soon as we stopped in order to look for water . . . and did not make an appearance all night."

Oct. 21.

line east to Santa Fe. Although there was no way of knowing what lay ahead, spirits were lifted knowing that home was now almost directly to the east. The riders wound their way through a maze of bluffs, arroyos and large boulders. To save time and because of the nature of the provisions they had traded for, they did not cook, rather each man was provided with a few dry cactus pear cakes, a handful of seeds and a few piñon nuts. The seeds caused a growing thirst and the water cask was soon empty. All through that day the men rode on, craving water but finding none. Camp was made and Olivares, who was suffering the most, rode ahead in search of a water hole. Darkness came and he did not return. He " . . . *did not make an appearance all night; this caused us plenty of worry. Today 26 miles."* Because of the roughness of the terrain a beacon fire would have done little good. The dry-mouthed travelers turned to their blankets and waited for dawn.

Chapter 6

A CANYON AND
⊰ A RIVER ⊱

A fingernail sliver of moon hung above the eastern horizon. Dawn was casting just enough light to load packs
and saddle the horses. It was October 22, 1776, and without
the protection of their sleeping blankets the cold morning air
met no resistance from the mens' thin summer clothing. They
moved out towards the northeast in the same direction that
Olivares had disappeared the evening before. He hailed them
five miles later and led them to a shrunken, algae-slick rain
water pool that contained only enough for the men to drink
— nothing was left with which to fill the water cask. The
thirsty animals were kept down wind so they would not catch
the scent. It proved a difficult day, " . . . *very rocky besides having many gulches.*"

They rode into the evening still looking for water for
themselves and the restless horses and mules. Finally, from a
high ridge and just after dark, they spotted three fires burning
on the plain below. Andrés and Joachín had ridden ahead earlier to scout for water. These had to be their signal fires. The
riders continued through the darkness towards the flickering
lights. Drawing within hailing distance, Miera yelled out a
deep-throated greeting. From the fires came cries of fear and
sounds of panic. They had unwittingly approached an Indian

*"It was already dark when we reached these camps, and the Indians .
. . became so much alarmed that . . . most of them ran away.*
Oct. 22. Forty miles west of the Colorado River.
Detail from a roadside monument in Arizona.

encampment, but mixed in with the commotion could be
heard the voices of Andrés and Joachín. The expedition
stopped and waited. Andrés soon stepped out of the dark and
led them into the camp.

He and Joachín had found this small temporary village
shortly before dark and were trying to explain who they were
when the inhabitants heard Miera's booming voice. All had
fled except for three men and two women who cowered
behind the Laguna boy pleading with him for protection.
Domínguez brought the riders to a halt outside the ring of
flickering firelight, dismounted and slowly advanced. When
he reached Joachín he tenderly embraced the young Laguna
and then held out his arms to the wide-eyed individuals cow-
ering behind him. No one moved. Domínguez stood quietly,
his arms still outstretched, open palms upward, his eyes

moving gently from one frightened face to the next. Finally, one of the men took several cautious steps forward. He reached out and touched the padre's hand and felt living flesh. This was no ghost, just another man. The five called out for their friends and families. Silent, shadowy forms emerged from the darkness. Only then did Domínguez signal for the rest of the men to dismount, leave the animals where they were and approach the center of the camp.

A short time later the entire expedition was crowded around one of the fires where they divided two roasted jackrabbits into thirteen portions. The bony carcasses did not go far but every bite was savored. Afterwards each man was given a small handful of piñon nuts. Even more welcome was a clay water jar that had been handed around — several times. Joachín made it known to his new friends, a band of desert-dwellers closely related to the Paiute people, that the horses and mules also needed water. Two of the village men helped guide the animals through the dark to a small pool fed by a living spring, less than a quarter mile away. At last the camp was asleep — with the exception of Captain Miera and a desert-burned old man.

The Spaniard had eaten his scant portion of the meal only to have his stomach react with gut-wrenching pain. The old one led him to a nearby brush hut and there knelt over him and began to chant. Whatever gods the man called on, Miera did not know or care. He was willing to try anything to ease the pain. The repetitious chant droned on, mesmerizing and soothing. The agony eased and the exhausted captain dropped into the oblivion of sleep.

Towards morning Domínguez himself fell ill. Dawn came and others were feeling similar symptoms. Days of eating little more than handfuls of seeds and cactus fruit had taken a toll. The villagers were beginning to show anxiety about the ill

Spaniards. Escalante knew these people often attributed illness to demons. If that was what they were thinking now, he had to act. He gave orders for the horses and mules to be driven some distance away to graze in a deep arroyo. The weakest horse was kept behind and its throat cut. Whatever apprehensions had been present concerning ill Spaniards quickly disappeared. The excited desert dwellers crowded around to watch the butchering operation. The carcass was badly emaciated from weeks of exertion and poor diet but even so, most of the Indians had never seen so much meat at one time. Runners were sent to spread the good news and other Indians began to appear. Soon, eager, dirt-encrusted hands were reaching out for strips of the dark, half-cooked meat. The bones were roasted and broken open to extract the marrow. The intestines were squeezed free of their contents, cut into strips and toasted over the fire before being devoured. Liver, heart, lungs, brain and nearly everything else disappeared except a portion of one hind quarter which had been wrapped in the hide and placed inside an empty pannier. The desert dwellers had participated in a fine feast.

A bond was beginning to grow between themselves and their visitors. Bellies full, the Indians indicated they had food to exchange for strips of colored ribbons like those tied into Joaquín's hair. When the last trade had been made, two panniers had been nearly filled with a bushel of piñon nuts. The thirst inducing and stomach cramping seeds the expedition had traded for earlier were presented as a gift to the host camp which accepted them gratefully.

Through the course of the day, villagers were questioned about the river crossing. Their answers were conflicting but they all indicated the canyon itself was not more than thirty miles towards the northeast.

By the following morning Domínguez and Miera were well enough to ride again. Escalante had been told about the earlier healing ceremony that had been held for Captain Miera. The young Franciscan was not pleased — neither was Domínguez. Prior to riding out at mid-morning, and with a considerable crowd of people gathered around to see them off, the two priests launched into a joint sermon — as much for the benefit of their own followers as for their new friends. *"We proclaimed the Gospel to them, decrying and explaining to them the wickedness and futility of their evil customs, most especially with regard to the superstitious curing of their sick. We made them understand that they should seek help in their troubles only from the one and true God . . . ."* Afterwards it was asked if the people would be willing to invite other padres to come and teach them. The answer was so emphatically affirmative that the priests opened a trade pack and gave each person present a short piece of colored ribbon. Never had these Kaibab desert dwellers been so sorry to see anyone leave. The travelers had brought not only food but they were also exceedingly generous with their gifts.

One of the older Paiute men had agreed to lead the Spaniards to the river crossing and after a final exchange of good-byes, the expedition turned towards the northeast. Less than two miles from the camp, the new guide bolted off through the brush. A disgusted Escalante wrote, *"Our thoughtless companions wanted us to make him keep his word by force, but we, understanding his reluctance, let him go freely away."* Escalante believed they had enough information to find the ford themselves. Five miles later the riders changed direction as they had been instructed — now towards the southeast where they traversed " . . . *sandy and troublesome country* . . . ."

Camp was made at the southeast corner of Paria Plateau which towered more than 2,000 feet above their flickering camp fires. There was no water or forage that night for the stock. The men fared better. They had the meat saved from the butchered horse. It was cut into strips, portioned out and roasted. After their meager meal the men sat close to the fires cracking and eating piñon nuts. The night was noticeably cooler. Winter was extending its reach into the desert country, still there was an air of anticipation in the camp that evening. Tomorrow, if the Paiutes were right, they would reach the river, and hopefully find the crossing.

The following morning, less than three miles from camp, the expedition saw the first side canyons, all dry and impressively deep. The riders were forced northward to avoid the fissures. A halt was called midafternoon and camp was made at the base of high cliffs that ran north and south and blocked out the western horizon. Cottonwoods grew around a small spring which supported enough grass to keep the stock from wandering. Cisneros, restless as always, continued north to see

"This afternoon we saw the embankments and cliffs of the river's box canyon . . . which give the impression of a lengthy row of structures."
Oct. 24. Southwest of Lee's Ferry.

"We took the box channel of an arroyo in search of water for the horse herds, which by now were exhausted from thirst."

Oct. 25. Approaching the Colorado River.

"In the afternoon . . . Cisneros . . . returned . . . with the welcome news of his now having reached the river . . . but saying that he did not know if we could be able to get across . . . ."

Oct. 25. South of Lee's Ferry at Navajo Bridge.

what lay ahead. He returned near midnight. Beneath the light of a nearly full moon and from a high ridge he had glimpsed the waters of the Colorado, imprisoned between the walls of a deep gorge. The vertical walls of rock were not traversable for men, much less horses and mules. Cisneros believed the crossing had to be further up-stream.

October 26 brought with it a hint of frost. Camp was struck and the water cask was filled. Hopefully that night they would drink from the river. Cisneros took the lead only to realize eight miles from camp that he was not on the same trail he had followed the previous night. The land had looked different in the dark. He shrugged, turned his horse more to the east in hopes of picking up his tracks, and the expedition rode on. Five miles south of present day Lee's Ferry, the sandstone they had been riding on gave way to deep sand. Horses and

"We continued . . . with excessive difficulty because the horse herds sank up to their knees in the dirt . . . ."
Oct. 26. Two miles west of the Colorado River.

mules sank past their hocks, but three miles later they could see, " . . . *El Río Grande de los Cosninas*."

The Spaniards gazed downward at the turbulent waters of the Colorado. It was obvious no horse or mule could cross at that location. Cisneros turned his horse north where he found his tracks from the night before.

A short time later the riders came to the shallow waters of the Paria River flowing from the northwest and emptying into the great river below. They followed it down to where its waters mingled with those of the Colorado. Two strong swimmers stripped naked, secured their shirts and trousers around their heads, turban-fashion, and waded in some distance above the confluence. *"It was so deep and wide that the swimmers, in spite of their prowess, were barely able to reach the other side, leaving in midstream their clothing, which they never saw again."*

The swift current had carried the swimmers nearly a quarter mile down river before they had been able to reach the opposite bank. Wet, naked and shivering in the cold air they rested for a time then hiked back to a point above where they had first entered and again plunged into the current. After a second bone chilling swim, they were greeted with a fire and spare clothing.

The Paiutes had assured Domínguez and Escalante this was the condition they would find all along the river — except at a single crossing where the river slowed and widened, and where a man could wade across in water that came no higher than his waist. The sun had already dipped below the horizon. Camp was made beside a sandstone cliff. The stock was turned loose to forage.

At daybreak scouts set out on foot, up and down river, carrying a few handfuls of piñon nuts. A third party climbed to the rim of the west cliffs and also traveled north. Those who remained behind gathered driftwood and built a raft. It

"A wood raft was put together . . . , but since the poles used for pushing it did not touch bottom . . . it thrice came back to the shore it had left."

Oct. 28. Lee's Ferry.

might be possible to ferry men, saddles and supplies across, and let the horses and mules swim. A short distance into the waters, with fifteen foot poles, the rafters discovered they could not touch bottom. The crew regained the shore and allowed the raft to drift away in the current.

Two days passed before the scouts returned from down river. They had not found a crossing. Instead, the canyon deepened rapidly, its vertical walls so narrow in places, the surging waters touched the cliffs on both sides. The crossing had to be further north.

That afternoon Escalante caught up on his journal entries and ended with, " *. . . the piñon nuts and other things we had brought had run out, we ordered another horse killed."* Twice more the sun made its journey across the great gorge. The scouts from up river had returned except Cisneros who finally walked into camp the following afternoon, exhausted, weak from hunger but believing he had found the ford.

"The river . . . has quicksands on either bank, in the likes of which we could lose all . . . of the horse herd."

Oct. 27.

The next morning, horses and mules with six days of rest behind them, began the climb up the north side of the Canyon of the Paria. Escalante grimly referred to the campsite they left behind as *"San Benito de Salsipuedes."* A place of punishment from which escape is difficult.

The journey out of the canyon was far more strenuous than anything they had encountered in many days but by late afternoon the expedition had gained the heights. They were only two and a half miles from their previous camp. Spirits were low, animals exhausted and that evening, November 1, the temperature began to drop. *"This afternoon from sundown to seven in the morning, we were exceedingly cold."* The men huddled together that night, wrapped in their ponchos and blankets.

The next morning packs were secured and saddle cinches given an extra tug, and for the next three hours men and animals climbed a second incline then wound their way through *"extremely difficult stretches and most dangerous ledges."* To their immediate right lay the rotted edges of eroded rim-rock cliffs. One slip on one crumbling ledge would mean instant death. Eventually they were able to work back from the rim and began a gradual descent to the north. Rock gave way to loose sand that sucked and pulled with every step. Two hard days of travel had netted them less than eight miles but that evening they did find pools of brackish rain water and pasture for their exhausted animals.

The next day proved no better. Terrain forced the expedition back towards the southeast and by midmorning they could again see the waters of the Colorado, 1,700 feet below them, this time flowing around a great bend. In places it appeared that the cliffs might be negotiated down to the river. It was here that Cisneros believed a crossing might be made.

He pointed to the mouth of a small canyon that appeared to exit up and out the east side of the main gorge. Two mules were led down to test the route but less than half way the animals stopped. The route was open but the beasts refused to go further without their companions, now out of sight on top of the rim. Their packs were removed and one was persuaded to climb back to the top. The second remained stranded on a narrow shelf, unwilling to go up or down. From a high point of rocks further north on the rim, it was observed that if all the animals could be taken to the bottom and if the bend did not provide a crossing place, there might be a way back out of the gorge further upstream. Juan Domingo, the runaway from Abiquiú, who had swum the river earlier, volunteered to climb down and test the crossing then hike into the canyon on the opposite side. He would find out if it could be used for an exit up the east side of the gorge. He was told to return before nightfall, then quickly disappeared below the cliffs. An hour later he was swimming the current, this time his shirt, trousers and moccasins tied securely to his back. He reached the far bank and entered a side canyon on the east side. He was soon out of sight.

It was then that Lucrecio Muñíz advanced a new idea. He would take his horse down, swim the river and link up with Domingo somewhere in the canyon. If the route was open, he would ride far enough back to build a smoky fire to signal for the rest of the expedition to begin the decent so the stock would be at the bottom and watered before dark. To give his horse every advantage he removed the saddle and led the mount down past the stranded mule. He had stripped to his shirt and moccasins and around his neck carried a pouch containing flint, steel and charred cloth with which to start a fire. He made a safe crossing, his horse swimming strongly, then he too disappeared into the mouth of the canyon on the east bank. The afternoon sun began its drop towards the horizon. Eager eyes continued to watch the eastern side of the gorge for smoke — but none appeared. From the ledge below the cliffs the stranded mule called repeatedly to its companions above. The water cask was empty. Two men made the climb down to the river and struggled back up the cliffs two hours later with the dripping water container suspended between them on a long pole of driftwood. The last of the horsemeat was roasted and rationed out. Finally, most took to their blankets, a few still keeping watch towards the east

"We went down the other side through cliff-lined gorges as we headed north . . . into an arroyo which had water running in places . . . .There was also pasturage here, and so we halted."

Nov. 2.

but all they saw was a bright moon, three days past full, rising above the eastern rim of the dark canyon where Domingo and Lucrecio had disappeared.

November 4 dawned quietly. The moon had already set below the west horizon. The air was sharp and cold. There was still no sign of Juan Domingo or Lucrecio Muñíz. If they did not show up by mid-morning the expedition would descend the same route Lucrecio had followed the previous day. An advance party was sent to mark the easiest path for the animals. It returned two hours later with a quantity of cactus pads and shriveled hackberries picked from trees near the river. The needles on the pads were burned off and the charred outer covering peeled away. The sticky pulp inside was eaten. The hackberries were boiled in water to make a weak bittersweet tea. It was a poor breakfast but better than nothing. Of more pressing importance were the animals. They had to be watered. By mid-morning the expedition was snaking its way down the ledges. The stranded mule greeted its mates and joined the descent. They reached the river by mid-day. Several horses had been unable to maintain their footing over loose rocks and one was badly injured. Its throat was cut and the unfortunate beast had to be butchered where it fell.

Just before evening Juan Domingo reappeared at the mouth of the canyon on the opposite bank of the river. Some time later, dressed in dry clothing, huddled close to the fire, and between mouthfuls of horsemeat, he told what he had found. The side canyon extended a considerable distance towards the east and while men could climb out, it would be impossible for the animals. Lucrecio, having discovered moccasin tracks, left his horse when it could go no further and climbed above the rim to explore further north in hopes he could find either a trail or another side canyon the animals could exit from. Domingo had not seen him again. Late that night deep in the canyon beside the dark, gurgling waters of the river, the men saw the light of a moon, still hidden by the east cliffs, casting shadows on the ledges they had so laboriously descended that day. They knew there would be no escape across the river at this place. They would continue to follow the river upstream, hoping that somewhere, they would find a way across or a way back up the west cliffs. An unspoken thought rested heavily on the mind of each man. Perhaps they had descended into a trap from which there would be no escape, at least for the stock.

"Today we stopped . . . close to a multitude of earthen embankments, small mesas, and peaks of red earth which looked like the ruins of a fortress . . . ."
Nov. 2. Between Lee's Ferry and the crossing.

Morning came and still no Lucrecio. Somewhere, across the river and on the opposite rim was a man wearing only a shirt and moccasins, and who had not eaten for two days. Had he injured himself? Had he met the owners of those unidentified moccasin tracks? Had they killed him? Domínguez left Lucrecio's brother, Andrés, behind with a small quantity of roasted horse meat and the missing man's trousers, poncho and a blanket. He was to remain and keep watch until evening and then, if Lucrecio had not returned, Andrés was to rejoin his companions.

The rest of the expedition saddled up and was soon winding its way around the bend north along the river bank. The canyon floor began to pull away from the water, the cliffs became less imposing and by late afternoon the expedition had worked its way back to the top of the west rim. The day had netted only seven and a half miles of travel up river but a campsite was located that had water and grass. All that day riders had kept a watch on their backtrail hoping to see the Muñíz brothers but to no avail. Heavy clouds had been gathering through the afternoon and shortly after dark it began to rain.

It was still raining at daybreak when Andrés rode into camp — alone. He had remained on watch all the previous day and had left only when it grew dark. He had ridden through the night to reach camp, but was unwilling to go further unless he knew his brother's fate. Reprovisioned with more horse meat, he disappeared into the mist, this time intent on swimming the river and finding out what had happened to his younger brother.

Near mid-morning the rain ceased only to be replaced by a freshening wind from the north. Before noon, rain struck again, this time bringing with it large hailstones. There was no protection on the open rim of the canyon. Jagged bolts of lightening scattered fire among nearby rocks followed by instantaneous " . . . *horrendous thunder claps* . . . ." Horses reared and plunged, mules brayed in white-eyed terror. The men turned to the Virgin Mary to " . . . *implore some relief for us, and God willed for the tempest to end.*" The hail ceased. The bolts of fire found new targets further south. The last echoes of thunder reverberated through the gorge below and then it was silent, except for the continuing rain. Gullies that had been dry the day before now ran water. Solid earth gave way to hoof-sucking mud. A halt was called early and a noon camp was made. It was too wet for fires and cold enough that patches of hail refused to melt.

Cisneros, unwilling to waste daylight, rode on alone to explore. He returned midafternoon — convinced he had found both the ford and a way down the west cliffs. If the route was open and if he had found the ford, the opposite bank was nothing more than a steep incline. The way east was open. Domínguez, not trusting the optimism in Cisneros' voice, sent him back with two companions to get their opinion. The three returned at dark all sharing Cisneros' optimism.

"We went down into a dry arroyo . . . passing over a brief shelf of soft white rock."
Nov. 5. A few miles south of the Colorado River crossing.

The two Muñíz brothers rode into camp not long after. Andrés had found Lucrecio following the expedition's trail earlier that day. The latter had been almost three days without clothing, shaking from the cold and weak from hunger. As for his attempt to find a way up and out of the canyon, that had been unsuccessful. He had climbed out of the side canyon on the east rim and had moved north on foot. He had found another canyon and then another. Each one led him further but Lucrecio kept believing that the next one might be passable for the stock. Although the expedition leaders were upset the young man had not followed his original instructions, they gave no reprimands. They understood how easy it was to believe that perhaps the next ridge, the next side canyon, might reveal a way out of their rock-walled prison. There was both laughter and fires that night, young Lucrecio was wearing trousers again, and tomorrow they would examine the site Cisneros was so optimistic about.

November 7 dawned warmer than it had been in several days. Domínguez, Escalante, Felipe and Juan Domingo were up at first light and rode north, across great sheets of weathered sandstone to the side canyon leading down into the main gorge. They left their horses at the rim and began the climb down. The descent was easy except for twenty feet of steeply angled sandstone a short distance below the rim. They were soon at the river's edge, half a mile downstream, where it was the widest. Juan Domingo stripped and waded in, slowly, carefully. The water came to his knees and then to his waist. He continued wading but the water came no higher. Finally, he stood on the opposite bank. They had found the ford. The only remaining obstacle was the sandstone decline near the top of the side canyon they would need to use to come down to the river. It was traversable for men on foot but the animals would need something more. They would need steps. Soft

"It became necessary to cut steps with axes on a stone cliff."

Nov. 7.

sandstone was soon giving away beneath the blades of hatchets and axes. Steps more than three feet wide were cut deep enough for an animal to maintain a solid footing. The horses and mules had been relieved of saddles and packs on the canyon rim directly above where Juan had waded the river and then the herd was brought the half mile north to the side canyon where it would descend. The most sure-footed mules were led down first. Men held their breaths. If the animals would descend the steps, the rest of the way down would be easy. With almost no hesitation the lead mule negotiated its way downward. Once it had reached the bottom, a second was led to the edge, then another and another. Enough distance was kept between each animal that if one lost its footing and fell, it would not crash into the one in front. It took nearly an hour to bring the herd down to the river but every animal made it safely.

Meanwhile the rest of the expedition began lowering saddles, packs and gear down the cliffs above the ford. An hour before sunset every man, every horse and mule and all the equipment they carried were on the east bank of the Colorado River. The exuberance of the moment was overwhelming. Thirteen days had been spent trying to find the crossing and now it was behind them. After the last rider emerged from the shallows, the entire expedition spent the next several minutes " . . . *praising God our Lord and firing off some muskets in demonstration of the great joy we all felt in having overcome so great a problem . . . .*"

The animals were driven to a grass-covered section of riverbank to graze and camp was made. Escalante committed to his journal details of where and how the crossing should be approached from the west. He did not want the next band of travelers to suffer as his companions had through the " . . . *detours, inclines, and bad stretches.*"

After dark Captain Miera, to better mark the location of the crossing, took a latitude reading from the North Star. Tomorrow they would resume their journey towards the southeast and home to Santa Fe.

No one would forget this day or this victory, and enduring evidence was left behind that an expedition had passed that way. The steps cut into the sandstone rock, would still be visible nearly two centuries later before disappearing beneath the rising waters of Lake Powell.

Chapter 7

THE
⚔ STARVING TIME ⚔

The men awoke the morning of November 8 still retaining much of the exuberance they had felt the evening before. They were finally free of the great rock gorge and the river beneath its high cliffs. Home suddenly seemed closer than since the journey had begun. The stock had spent much of the night grazing in hock-high grass that grew below the camp. The ordeal the animals had faced showed plainly. Bone protruded where once there had been muscle and fat. A few more days in the canyon might have meant the end for many of the horses. The mules were better able to survive under such harsh conditions.

Scouts had already walked to the top of the rise that led to the east rim. They found no surprises. It would be an easy climb. The last pieces of juiceless horsemeat were roasted over a fire of river driftwood and unceremoniously eaten. The men were able to complain a little again. How good it would have been to have had some salt with their breakfasts. But it was a good-natured complaining. The canyon was behind them.

Strung out in the usual order of march, the expedition soon climbed upwards and towards the morning sun. At the top of the eastern canyon ridge they turned south squeezing between a high, slender butte and the rising cliffs of the river gorge now on their right. For a little more than a mile they rode silently, watching their former adversary flowing hundreds of feet below. The river seemed more benign now, its sounds muted by distance even as the protesting waters were being constrained more tightly between the cliffs. Near the next bend the men turned their horses towards the east again to avoid a line of buttes and mesas. The river dropped from sight for the final time, the sound of its waters faded away. Sandstone shelves similar to the ones the expedition had traversed for two weeks on the opposite side of the river gave way to patches of earth and stunted stands of juniper and piñon pine. The expedition crossed, for the second time, into the future state of Arizona. About noon a shout went up from the lead riders — ahead was an Indian trail.

The men continued towards the southeast on the trail they had picked up, and saw what became an abundance of moccasin prints, some reasonably fresh. Thirteen sets of eyes kept watch on the horizon, but the only movements were

"After going three leagues over good terrain we halted, even without water, because there was good pasturage for the horse herds.
Nov. 11. Four days after crossing the Colorado.

those of a few wild desert sheep. It was the first game the men had seen in weeks but not one of the creatures approached within musket range. Towards late afternoon the land began to change again. Twisted and tilted formations of layered sandstone, many the size of a house, jutted upwards out of the earth. Time and erosion had accentuated each lamination making it appear as if one stone layer had been stacked upon the next before all were squeezed and cemented together. Occasionally the horses and mules had to work their way through beds of foot-sucking sand. Some of the weaker animals struggled to keep up so the pace was slowed. Near sunset a halt was called beneath the base of a magnificent cliff. They made camp early where " . . . *there was good pasturage and plenty of rainwater. Today 16 miles."*

The weakest and most emaciated horse was killed that evening and skinned out. It had been an obedient animal that had carried its rider without complaint. In the cooling evening air, steam rose from the shrunken muscles and a featureless heap of entrails that lay nearby. Butchering knives soon had the carcass reduced to skeletal form, which would be torn apart, picked clean and scattered by scavengers in the days to come. The hide would be saved to re-sole moccasins and repair panniers. The bones would bleach beneath a relentless sun before flaking and crumbling away.

A quantity of meat was roasted over the cook fires and everyone ate in silence. Soon afterwards the camp grew silent. The men huddled together for sleep, in twos and threes, shifting and adjusting their bodies and blankets to seal out the probing chill of night.

Two hours into a new morning the Indian trail they had followed the previous day disappeared in a series of sandstone benches. Ahead lay more cliffs and high ridges. The expedition turned up a canyon towards the northeast but after less than six miles of travel was forced to stop at the base of a cliff. It was decided to make camp and send scouts out on foot to search for the vanished trail. They returned with news they had located a camp of Paiutes. When they tried to make contact, the inhabitants fled, carrying with them their meager belongings and food baskets. They left only brush shelters and dying fires. Andrés and Joaquín were taken to the site but despite their greetings of friendship the people of the abandoned camp remained hidden in the high cliffs. The Spaniards returned to their own camp and prepared to spend the night, making a great show of roasting slices of horsemeat and eating it in plain view — in the effort to coax someone down. The gesture was in vain.

Before sunup Andrés and Joaquín took Domínguez and Escalante to the abandoned Paiute camp in hopes the blue-robed priests might stir enough curiosity to initiate conversation. The Paiute people were still hidden in the rocks above. The expedition leaders remained in sight but well back while the interpreter and Indian boy " . . . *cajoled them for more than two hours* . . . " Five men then warily made their way down only to flee again when the two priests began to approach. The padres retreated. Andrés and Joaquín approached the cliffs alone. A lone figure stepped from behind a rock high above. In sign language he told the pair that his band had little food — nothing worth stealing. Another Paiute came into view. This one spoke. He gave directions how to relocate the trail lost the previous day. His communication ended with several Spanish words.

Escalante had been listening and his breath caught in his throat." . . . *El Pueblo de Oraibe in Moqui.*" Oraibe was 100 miles northwest of Zuñi, Escalante's own mission station! Oraibe was where Father Garcés had posted the letter that had reached Santa Fe the previous July! Escalante had visited the town himself just a year before that. Excited, he yelled for Andrés to ask how many days it would take to journey to Oraibe. The interpreter repeated the question, but the entire band of Paiutes were already vanishing above the lip of the cliff.

The four returned to camp. It was past noon. Scouts were sent out with the directions that had been given for exiting the canyon and relocating the trail. If the Indians had spoken truthfully about the trail then surely they had spoken the truth about Oraibe. Camp was moved a mile up the canyon where there was better grazing. The afternoon began to fade.

Escalante recorded the events of the morning in his journal still turning over in his mind a single word — *"Oraibe."* At sunset the scouts returned. The directions they had been given were accurate and not two hours away they had found where the trail continued towards the southeast.

The expedition moved out the next morning at first light and seven miles later picked up the path. At one point, where it disappeared into a rocky canyon, earlier travelers had marked it with piles of stones. Soon the expedition was at the confluence of Navajo Creek and Kaibito Wash. They continued upwards towards the canyon rim. At times the trail grew perilous and narrow, passable for men on foot but less so for

"We halted, even if without water, because there was good pasturage for the horse herds and plenty of firewood to ward off the severe cold."

Nov. 11.

horses and mules. One by one the beasts were coaxed up a shelf so narrow that panniers had to be removed from the animals and carried by hand. After an hour of sweat-breaking labor, the

expedition stood on the canyon rim looking at the backtrail —
today covered with the waters of Lake Powell.

*"We started out . . . along the course mentioned, and over good
terrain of woods and abundant pastures."*

Nov. 14. Fifty miles northwest of Oriabi.

The Indian trail pointed south-southeast and good time
was made over level terrain. Camp was made that evening in
a place where there was adequate forage for the animals but no
water except what was in the cask. After sundown the temperature began to drop, but the abundant amount of collected
wood made it possible to keep fires burning well into the
morning hours. Even so, sleepers shifted and turned. The sides
of their bodies next to the fire grew too warm, the sides that
faced away became too cold.

The following day it was decided to separate into two
groups. Half of the riders were in their saddles shortly after
first light, leaving with half of the pack mules and loose
horses. Their companions followed a short time later. It was
hoped that six or seven men would be less intimidating should

they encounter other groups of local inhabitants. They rode through the cold dawn, still wrapped in their sleeping blankets and huddled in their saddles. There had been nothing to eat that morning. The last of the horsemeat had disappeared the night before.

Shortly after the morning sun had crossed its quarter point, both groups rode by several deserted brush shelters, and saw evidence that domestic cattle and horses had been in the area the previous summer. Not far from the brush huts was a small spring and a substantial pool of water. The ice had been broken by the advance riders, who had drank and watered their stock but had taken care not to roil the water for those following. The second group of riders drank, the cold water partially numbing the sharp ache of hunger that now gripped their bellies. Afterwards they let their own animals crowd around to drink. The men stamped numb feet, swung their arms round and round, and clapped their hands to bring back circulation and a little warmth. The second party continued on in the tracks of the lead group.

The land was changing — ever larger formations of sandstone jutted skyward out of the ground. Scattered stands of stunted juniper and piñon huddled together, sharing the meager nourishment they found in the red, water-starved earth.

A weak winter sun began its descent towards the west. It had given no heat all day. Immobile knees ached, feet grew numb, Captain Miera shivered violently. The old soldier, still at war with his stomach, had been eating even less than his companions. He rode silently, head down, numb fingers entwined through loose reins, both hands gripping the horn of his saddle. He made no request to stop. Afternoon shadows were blending with those of a coming night. The advance party was not far ahead, hopefully with fires waiting. There would be no food but at least water could be heated and herbs gathered to make a warming tea for the ailing captain.

Warm fires were waiting but no water. The advance party had the mule that carried the water cask, and no one had filled it that morning at the spring. Hot anger boiled into curses. Not a single bite of food had been consumed that day and some could not decide which was worse, the agony of thirst or the pains of hunger. A few cut pieces of the still wet horsehide they had saved and roasted them over the fire. The charred results smelled like burned hair and tasted worse. There was more cursing. Escalante, bitter and frustrated, wrote that evening, *"Because of their carelessness we suffered great thirst tonight."* Miera, who would have benefited the most from drinking something warm, had to settle for a place close by one of the fires, sheltered by the bodies and blankets of his companions.

November 13 dawned cold and deathly still. Winter had arrived and it brought with it the specter of starvation. There was a rallying point that morning when the captain stirred from his blankets, and with a certain bravado, proclaimed himself ready for another day in the saddle. The idea to continue on in two separate groups was abandoned. The men would ride together again. Five miles later they found a small water hole, ice covered, but the cold water beneath was the sweetest anyone could remember. This time the cask was filled and the stock allowed their turn. In a few minutes nothing remained of the puddle but trampled shards of muddy ice. It had not been enough but down the trail they found a second pool. Again the horses and mules crowded in to drink.

While the stock was watering, a porcupine was spotted slowly making its way through the brush. After a few blows from a hastily acquired club, the creature was deposited in an empty pannier and the men bantered ideas back and forth as to how the animal should be cooked that night. An hour before sunset camp was made five miles north or present day Tuba City, Arizona. Escalante wrote, " . . . *the porcupine shared among so many only served to whet the appetite. Hence we ordered another horse deprived of its life. It was something we had not done sooner because we had expected to find provisions in some Cosnina camp . . . today fifteen miles.*"

"We caught a porcupine today, and here we tasted flesh of the richest flavor."

Nov. 13.

Even with the periodic infusions of horsemeat it was evident the men were beginning to starve. Their faces were becoming increasingly gaunt. Simple exertions such as saddling a horse or loading a mule were becoming more difficult and time consuming. A quiet desperation was beginning to settle in with both Domínguez and Escalante. What if the path they were on did not lead to Oraibe?

The following morning the trail gradually began to swing from the south back towards the southeast. The change in direction was comforting to Miera. In terms of latitude the expedition was almost due west of Santa Fe, but the question remained — how far? The land was becoming ever more dry and desolate. Narrow, shallow canyons cut ragged gashes through the red earth. In places there were shallow dunes of sand alternating with deep trenches scooped out by the wind — almost grave-like in appearance. Short, sheared off buttes broke the monotony of the horizon.

That afternoon, they saw several head of cattle, roaming free but obviously not wild. A shout went up, muskets were primed and several prepared to ride out to intercept the beasts, but a sharp command from Domínguez ordered them to hold their line of march. The order was met with vigorous protest. Escalante came to the defense of the expedition leader. He knew that the Hopi people of the villages around Oraibe kept cattle and horses. Perhaps other people did too. Either way, these had to be Indian cattle and to kill one without permission, and without paying for it would be taken as a sign of hostility. The men continued to argue. Perhaps these were runaways and if so that made them public property. The priests countered. Suppose they were observed killing a cow that was not theirs, not only by God, but by those who owned the beast? What retribution would follow? Were the men in any condition to resist? The arguments died away but that evening the priests ordered the killing of another emaciated horse. The water cask was drained, the stock went thirsty, and Domínguez and Escalante were met with a cold silence from everyone except the ever-faithful Joaquín.

The mood of the men next morning had not changed. If anything it had grown worse. No one bothered to cut away the meat that remained on the horse carcass from the night before. It was left for the coyotes. To Escalante it was clear he and Domínguez were close to losing control. The men were worn down. Human reason was being replaced by animal instinct. Authority, custom, trust in God — were all in danger of collapsing.

The trail continued towards the southeast for more than seven miles through country now increasingly interspersed with buttes and mesas. Then it abruptly swung towards the east-northeast. In the distance more mesas began to break into view and north of those, a continuing line of high cliffs ran east and west. The miles fell away. Finally, someone spoke and pointed towards one of the distant mesas. It was marked by thin columns of smoke. The pace quickened, conversation became animated up and down the line. It had to be Oraibe!

With each mile the main trail became more evident. Smaller trails fed into it and all pointed towards the distant mesa now plainly crowned with tendrils of smoke.

Escalante strained his eyes hoping to see something familiar. He suddenly called out. It was Oraibe! Even though he had approached from the opposite direction the year before on his trip from Zuñi, he was certain it was Oraibe. A cheer went up from the men and shouts of thanksgiving to God.

Eighteen miles into that day's ride, the expedition stopped at the southern end of a high mesa. On top stood the village, " . . . *El Pueblo de Oraibe.*" It was not possible the expedition had approached unobserved, yet no one appeared on the pathway leading to the town above. The only sign of life was the smoke drifting skyward and dispersing into the chilly, evening air.

" . . . *we found a well-beaten trail and . . . arrived at the mesa of El Pueblo de Oraibe.*"

Nov. 16. Oraibe.

Domínguez dismounted and motioned Escalante and Cisneros to do the same. Cisneros would be needed since he spoke and understood the Navajo language, a tongue the Hopi were familiar with. Escalante led the way on foot up the incline towards the town above. Exhilaration was quickly dissolving into apprehension.

He remembered his visit the year before. He remembered the tension and veiled hostility. The people of Oraibe had once been home to a mission but during the revolt of 1680, they had killed the priest and burned the church. Subsequent attempts to rebuild the mission had been met with refusal. The people of Oraibe had their reasons. Escalante had heard the stories of earlier priests who had forced the men to drag timbers from across the desert to build the church. Infractions of ecclesiastical rules had been dealt with by the lash. Escalante had been told of these things. The people of Oraibe had long memories.

At the top of the pathway and out of sight from their companions, the three suddenly were faced with a sullen crowd of Hopi men. There was no way of knowing whether any carried weapons beneath their blankets. Escalante greeted the group warmly. Cisneros, in the Navajo tongue, interpreted. He related to the crowd that he, these two brothers, and others waiting below had come from the west on a long journey of many months. They needed food. They needed shelter from the cold.

"As we started to enter the pueblo a large number of Indians, big and small, surrounded us . . . one of them told us in Navajo not to enter the pueblo."

Nov. 16.

The villagers remained silent and impassive. Exasperated, Escalante motioned his two companions to follow and walked towards the home of the village headman. The crowd moved also, but only to block Escalante's path. In Navajo, one of the leaders spoke directly to Cisneros. There was no one in the village who wanted to see them. No one would extend them hospitality. They should leave.

For a brief moment there was silence. Rage welled up in Cisneros and he struck like a rattlesnake. He demanded to know why the Hopi were rebelling against their own custom of welcoming strangers? They had nothing to fear from a band of travelers who only wanted to trade for food and be on their way. His angry words were true. The hostile faces softened.

An old man came forward and offered his home, and the food from his hearth for that night. Escalante tenderly took their new host's bony frame into his arms and for a long moment, held him close.

Cisneros immediately made arrangements for the livestock and brought up the rest of their men. Around an inviting fire, the men enjoyed bread made from finely-ground corn meal, the first of many weeks. Everyone feasted and there was laughter.

When the last crumbs were disappearing the village headman came, accompanied by two advisors. They spoke to Cisneros. Enough supplies could be traded to see the party to the next pueblo, where additional provisions could be obtained. Trade was desirable for the people of Oraibe, but not at the risk of running short of food themselves. Winter had barely begun. The Spaniards understood. Domínguez presented gifts and was especially generous to the members of the host household. The village leaders left and body to body, on the crowded floor, twelve men and an Indian boy fell into an exhausted sleep.

Chapter 8

THE ROAD
⚔ TO ZUÑI ⚔

Shortly after dawn several women entered the crowded home of the old man. They picked their way around prostrate bodies still wrapped in their sleeping blankets, carrying a Hopi staple, fresh bread made from finely ground corn flour, beef tallow, and water, baked on hot, flat stones in paper-thin sheets. Bodies locked in the embrace of sleep began stirring as the aroma permeated the room. Feasting soon became the mistress of the moment. There was laughter too. Domínguez and Escalante knew the strain of the past few days had been banished with two good meals and a warm room to sleep in.

After breakfast most of the expedition walked down the steep path to tend the stock, gather their gear, and wait. They took their time knowing the villagers would be in no hurry to do any trading.

Midmorning came to the mesa top. The village leaders made their appearance carrying more bread — enough for two or three days. Domínguez glanced at Escalante who, in turn, gave a brief nod to Cisneros who would represent the expedition. Bread was of great value to the Spaniards but equally so were the trade goods spread before the Hopi traders. They were in no hurry. Time, on a winter day, was something they had an abundance of and there were other concerns. They were curious where the Spaniards had come from. Cisneros answered many questions and it was early afternoon before the final words had been spoken .

Domínguez made a lavish speech of thanks before they departed for the next village. Hopefully the expedition would find the same level of hospitality there as they had enjoyed at Oraibe. They were only a little more than 100 miles from Zuñi. In that town, Cisneros was the *"alcalde mayor."* They would no longer have to haggle for food or shelter.

The horses waited patiently at the foot of the mesa already saddled, panniers loaded onto the mules and the men impatient to move on. At the bottom of the pathway Escalante glanced back. Not a soul was in sight. Something did not seem right but he kept his concerns from Domínguez.

Nearly 100 years had passed since the people of Oraibe had risen up against their priest, killing him and burning the church. Escalante wondered what memories these people carried about that time? Had there been abuse of power and sexual improprieties or had this priest been blameless. Escalante had read parts of the report Domínguez had sent to Mexico City the previous July. Such behavior did not surprise him. He knew of similar happenings and while he could not and did not condone what some priests had done, and continued to do, he understood how such problems came about. To follow the path of poverty, chastity and charity, the Franciscans needed discipline and regimentation — not unlike that of a soldier. In addition, there were the difficulties of trying to teach and convert the Indian people, with their own long-established cultures, to the Gospel of Christ and the customs and mannerisms of Spaniards. These were people who eagerly accepted the technology of the eighteenth century — cloth and steel knives, but they had little desire to abandon the gods and ways that had sustained them through the centuries.

There was also the soul-searing isolation that mission personnel suffered at outlying villages — the priest at Oraibe had been the only Spaniard for 100 miles. As Escalante rode away that afternoon he thought about the last moments of that soldier of God. The Hopi had not admitted his murder. Their silence remained intact.

Somewhere, hidden beneath the winter sands of the desert, in unconsecrated ground, lay the bones of a Franciscan brother. The young priest glanced back a final time and said a prayer for the soul of a man he had never met, and for a people he wished he could better understand.

Escalante thought of the reception they would face at El Pueblo de Shongopavi, their next stop. Another worry was the lack of response he and Domínguez had received that morning when they asked for information about Santa Fe. The Oraibe elders either knew nothing or they were unwilling to share news they had. Their reply had been equally vague when Escalante asked about Zuñi.

The day was nearly spent. The late afternoon sun had cooled to little more than a dim sphere hanging above the western horizon. The two priests wore their pale blue woolen robes secured by a rope sash, broad, flat hats, moccasins and woolen capes. Their companions rode in their cotton trousers and shirts from the previous summer, ponchos over that and sleeping blankets wrapped around their shoulders and trailing past their knees. When necessary the head scarves they wore beneath their hats could be pulled down to cover their ears. Most had cut raw horsehide insoles and placed them inside their worn-out moccasins to keep their bare feet from contacting the ground. They had no socks. Immobile toes thrust into wooden stirrups grew numb riding through the cold. The same was true of a rider's knees. Each time a man dismounted he had to grasp the saddle horn and lower himself to the ground slowly where the prick of a thousand needles would shoot through his feet and lower legs. Until circulation returned walking was difficult and painful.

The village headman at Oraibe had earlier sent a runner ahead to announce the expedition's intentions to stop at Shongopavi now looming ahead on a mesa top. Any concerns Escalante had quickly disappeared as, " . . . *they welcomed us attentively, promptly giving us lodging.*"

The following morning the town was crowded with visitors from the neighboring villages of Shipaulovi and Moshongnovi. Some had come to satisfy their curiosity about the men who came from the great canyon to the west. Others wanted to trade. Trade they did, with the same agonizing slowness encountered the day before. Domínguez and Escalante were not in a position to deny their men provisions so patience prevailed. It was early afternoon before the last trade had been made.

The two priests thanked those who had come and began a joint sermon in Spanish, which Cisneros translated into Navajo. Problems began immediately when those who understood the latter refused to translate into the Moqui tongue which the majority of listeners understood. The village headman held up his hand for silence and, in Navajo, explained that it would be best if the priests waited until they were at Walpi where some of the inhabitants understood the Spanish tongue. There, he said, the preaching would be welcomed but, he himself had no wish to hear the words of the priests. They were willing to express friendship, but the people of Shongopavi did not want to hear words that might offend their own gods. With that said, orders were given to saddle up.

Before leaving the village the two priests presented a red woolen blanket to the man in whose household they had spent the previous night. The man handed it to his wife who pressed it tightly to her body. Her brother walked up, tore the blanket from her arms and threw it into the dirt at the Spaniards' feet, his face etched with murderous contempt. In the Moqui tongue he began to talk loudly, pointing first at Domínguez then to Cisneros. The Spaniards understood nothing. Finally the villager directed his attention to Escalante — this time in Navajo, which Cisneros translated. The angry one said he remembered Escalante from when the priest had passed through from the east. Now Escalante was back, from the west — attempting to undermine the gods. The people of Shongopavi wanted nothing from the Spaniards — not their gifts, not their ways, and not their religion. After a final contemptuous look, the speaker spun on his heel and walked away. The crowd followed, a few casting covetous looks at the blanket laying in the dirt. Cisneros and the two priests were alone. Escalante reached down, picked up the crumpled heap of cloth, refolded it and tucked it under his arm. The three made their way down the mesa to the horses.

It was nearly dark when the riders approached the mesa-top town of Walpi. Cisneros and the two priests dismounted and walked up the incline to the top of the mesa leaving their companions to wait below. They were greeted by a small crowd that included the village leaders and several visiting Tanos Indians. *"The Tanos and Walpis very joyfully received us, and they lodged us in the home of the . . . ritual headman where we spent the night."*

Early in the morning an unannounced visitor, deeply wrinkled, entered the quarters occupied by the expedition members. He carried the Spanish name of Pedro but he was a Tanos. His original village, south of Santa Fe, had been decimated by smallpox in 1749. The remaining inhabitants were too few to protect themselves from subsequent Comanche raids. For that reason it was abandoned. All but Pedro moved to the nearby pueblo of Santo Domingo. Pedro had resettled in Walpi and, because he was fluent in Spanish, had been delegated as spokesman that morning. He explained how, in recent months, the region had suffered attacks by Navajo raiders. Men had been killed. Women and children had been carried into captivity. It was unsafe to travel beyond the mesa towns. Pedro made his point quickly. Would the padres, when they reached Santa Fe, "*. . . beg the lord governor for some aid or defense against these foes?*" Domínguez and Escalante immediately asked that a council be called to discuss the matter. It was clear now why they had been welcomed so enthusiastically.

A council was called for the following morning and runners were sent to notify the six neighboring pueblos. Old Pedro spent much of the day exalting in his new position. He wanted to accompany the priests on to Santa Fe, and to speak to the governor himself. "*We answered him by saying that we would most gladly take him along . . . but that . . . it was necessary that each of the six pueblos dispatch someone in authority.*"

November 19 dawned late, the weak winter sun held captive behind a heavily overcast sky. The air felt heavy and wet. A storm was coming. Representatives from all six pueblos arrived near midmorning including "*. . . ritual headmen and war captains of these pueblos . . . .*" Pedro translated what the priests had to say into the Moqui tongue. Another Spanish-speaking Indian whom Escalante called Antonio the Twin simultaneously translated into the Tewa language. Both Domínguez and Escalante spoke. First they assured the council they intended to request aid in the fight against the Navajo. Then Domínguez told the council that "*. . . God alone is the one who can do everything and governs all, that they could not rid themselves of their suffering so long as they persisted in their infidelity and did not cease offending Him.*" If help was to come from the Spaniards, the people had to abandon their old gods. They had to embrace the teachings of the Church. What path did the people of Walpi and the surrounding pueblos wish to walk?

The council participants conferred among themselves and through Pedro and Antonio. Several individuals delivered their own orations. They wanted the help of Spanish arms but they did not want the teachings of the priests. To accept priests would mean the acceptance of the laws of the Spanish governor. They preferred their own laws.

Domínguez tried a different approach. *"If they submitted they would enjoy continual recourse to Spanish arms against all infidels who should war against them . . . ."* Again various council members spoke, this time expounding that any permanent alliance with the Spaniards might lead to a complete break in relations with neighboring pueblos. They could become isolated between two cultures, the Spanish on the east and other Indians to the west. That would be unacceptable.

Domínguez, direct and blunt, explained " . . . *that if they failed to submit to the Christian religion they would have to suffer without letup in hell . . . ."* Even this approach had no effect. " . . . *They replied that they solely desired our friendship but by no means to become Christians because the ancient ones had told them and counseled them never to subject themselves to the Spaniards."*

"Three times did we make our plea . . . by . . . demonstrating as vain and false the reasons they gave for their not converting to the faith."

Nov. 19.

The council was at an impasse. It was suggested that Pedro, the Tanos, be sent to talk to the governor, and represent the pueblos in requesting arms but the old man, having listened carefully to all that had been said refused, saying he had once been baptized into the Catholic Church and was fearful if he went to Santa Fe, he might never be allowed to return to Walpi. The council ended. The late afternoon sky was now obscured by falling snow. A disheartened Domínguez gave orders, weather permitting, the expedition should leave for Zuñi the following morning.

" . . . in the afternoon we set out from the pueblos of Walpi and
after going ten miles east by southeast, stopped to spend the night."
Nov. 20. Southeast of Oraibe.

Intermittent snow kept the Spaniards in Walpi until early the next afternoon, November 20, but by dark they were ten miles closer to Zuñi and camped at an abundant little spring. The skies remained overcast with light snow falling throughout the hours of darkness. Men huddled together for warmth but few slept. It was a miserable night, and at first light the animals were saddled and loaded. Hunched down and wrapped in their wet blankets the men took the trail. *"Today 19 miles."*

Zuñi was a few more days to the southeast. The stock was again beginning to wear down from the cold and miles of wet, hoof-sucking sand. Animals were beginning to miss their footing and stumble. No one wished to kill any more horses. The pace was slowed.

On the morning of November 22, it was decided the two priests, Joachín and two others would take the strongest mounts and ride ahead towards Zuñi. The rest would follow at whatever pace the remaining animals could maintain. It proved an exhausting day for the five but they covered almost thirty miles.

"We left the companions with what was left of the horse herds, which by now were all worn out."

Nov. 23.

Light snow continued, this time driven by a bitter wind that, had it not been at the riders' backs, would have made travel almost impossible.

The following day the trail veered due east. The snow intensified, and by late afternoon the temperature began to drop. Swirls of wind-driven flakes enveloped the riders from their left and visibility dropped to a few hundred yards. By now Escalante, in the lead, was on familiar ground.

That night the five huddled together beneath their blankets sleeping little, and wishing for the light of dawn. Horses, with no fat to insulate them, stared numbly into the featureless snow and darkness, tails turned to the wind. *"Tonight we suffered extreme cold. Today 31 miles, almost all to the east."*

"Here we rested a bit and continued east for two more leagues. The mounts gave out on us and we had to stop."

Nov. 22. Two days northwest of Zuñi.

At daybreak four men and a boy saddled up and continued in the direction of Zuñi but within two hours a halt was called. They were freezing to death. Needles of pain shot through moccasin clad feet as they touched the snow covered ground. They had to have a fire, and with great difficulty, one was built from dead brush that bare, wet hands had dragged in. Flames crackled in the cold air, bodies warmed, and the men ate enough bread to quiet the emptiness they were feeling in their bellies. They remounted and rode on. The day and the miles passed with agonizing slowness but finally, " . . . *we arrived extremely exhausted when it was already dark at the pueblo and mission of Nuestra Señora de Guadalupe de Zuñi. Today 32 miles.*"

Zuñi was small, barely three acres of stone and mud buildings huddled on the crest of a hill, but for the five exhausted riders it might have been the gates of heaven. For a long moment Father Silvestre Vélez de Escalante was held in the tight and joyous embrace of his co-pastor at the Zuñi mission, Father José Mariano Rosete y Peralta. Soon there were fires and food. Even the wet animals, for the first time since Santa Fe, were able to bed down in a stable. Though there was joy, the moment was tempered by the knowledge that the rest of the expedition was somewhere out in the snowy darkness.

Chapter 9

AN EARLIER
⊰ TIME ⊱

E scalante spent his first day in Zuñi preparing a letter to the governor. He briefly recounted the events of the preceding five months, explaining that the expedition planned to remain at the mission until the weather cleared, and the horses and men were in better condition to travel. Domínguez penned a similar letter to his superiors in Mexico City. Then they waited.

That afternoon the rest of the expedition rode in. Eight riders eased their cold, stiff bodies to the ground. Other hands, eager to help, led their emaciated mounts and the pack animals away to the warmth of the stables. Don Joaquín Laín and Don Pedro Cisneros quickly found the comfort of their own homes in Zuñi. Everyone else shared a hot meal at the mission which also provided sleeping quarters. Later, stretched out on untanned cowhides and rolled in their blankets, the travelers surrendered to the cumulative effects of five months in the saddle and weeks of exposure to winter weather.

The next morning the two letters penned the previous day were sent to Santa Fe by courier. In the days that followed, Domínguez and Escalante worked on the expedition journal, re-writing pages flawed or smudged by rain or snow. In places the entries reflected the times when hunger and frustration clouded the mind and literary abilities of the writer. These were left as they were — perhaps because there were so many. The document would be primarily for Governor Mendinueta, various officials in Mexico City, and perhaps members of the royal court in Spain.

Escalante also tended to ecclesiastical duties. He was still technically assigned as one of the two Zuñi ministers. Domínguez, not having been able to reach Zuñi during his inspection the preceding year, busied himself reading the mission records.

What he found pleased him. The settlement had been favored with adequate water and firewood. Pastures were abundant as were the livestock that grazed them. The church was constructed of adobe walls almost a yard thick, nearly 90 feet long by 27 feet wide, with a reach of 24 feet from the floor to a massive ceiling held in place by 36 massive wooden beams. Behind the altar was a large oil painting of Our Lady of Guadalupe, the patron saint of Mexico and her northern colonies since 1531. In his report Domínguez noted that, during the previous year, the church had consumed ten to twelve pounds of candles, and had used four jugs of wine to celebrate communion. Two bushels of wheat had been ground and used to bake the altar bread. No detail escaped the sharp-eyed Domínguez. He was slipping back into his roll as administrator and inspector.

A few days after the expedition's arrival the Zuñi people celebrated their most important event of the year, the ceremony of Shalako. Villagers gathered from the outlying pueblos in great numbers to participate in a pageant nearly as old and timeless as the pueblos themselves. Such celebrations were not condoned by the church but neither were they condemned or banned as they once had been. Although part of the area population around Zuñi embraced the Christian faith, many did not. Others adopted aspects of both

Christianity and their own native beliefs. Escalante was intimately familiar with the early history of the region, and he understood the resistance these people exhibited towards the teachings of the Church. It involved a sequence of events that had begun nearly two and a half centuries earlier.

Spanish troops under Nuñez de Guzmán had come across a small band of men in northern Mexico who had survived an expedition that had disappeared in the Gulf of Mexico several years earlier. For eight years these men had wandered across Texas into New Mexico and Arizona, then south into Mexico where they were finally found by Guzmán's soldiers. In Mexico City they were treated as heroes and talked of tribes they had met, some of which lived only for war and plunder. There were others with Christian hearts, but who had never known a priest. Stories were told about cities the survivors had heard about but had not seen — cities made of stone where people made cotton blankets and possessed quantities of turquoise. One of the survivors, a former black slave named Estéban, was convinced, more than his former companions, that had they traveled further north, they would have seen these places. His enthusiasm infected many of his listeners who compared his stories with similar accounts brought to Mexico by Indians themselves. One tale involved seven cities, somewhere far to the north that contained great quantities of gold, silver and precious gems.

Colonial officials saw enough merit in Estéban's stories to outfit a small exploration party under the leadership of Friar Marcos de Niza, an explorer priest who had helped blaze trails across parts of Central America and Peru some years earlier. Estéban, quite naturally, would be the expedition guide.

Friar de Niza and his band of followers rode northward, first along the western coastal regions of Mexico then northeast across the deserts of Arizona. When they approached the

Rio Grande Valley of New Mexico, Estéban insisted on traveling ahead of the main party to make contact with the pueblo people. He promised to send word back to de Niza about what he found. The former slave dressed himself in a plumed headdress, and a brightly colored robe adorned with tiny brass bells. He wrapped his wrists with jangling bracelets, and he carried a painted gourd rattle — the symbol of an Indian healer. Several attendants followed behind.

The first people he met greeted him with gifts of turquoise and the favors of young women. Estéban grew bold, demanding whatever he desired, making himself appear godlike to those he met. Then he reached an outlying village of the Zuñi people — Hawaikuh. Estéban's lusty appetite and his contemptuous attitude were not well received. There he was killed. Only two of his attendants escaped. In fear of their own lives, the rest of expedition returned to Mexico City. Friar de Niza, however, was convinced the Indians were hiding something of great value to have killed the dark-skinned Estéban. The expedition had come close enough to actually see one of the stone towns of New Mexico and were convinced these were a people who had riches.

Government officials were still cautious so they sent a second party under an experienced frontier officer named Melchoir Díaz in late November of 1539. Díaz rode with fifteen mounted soldiers and a small group of Indian porters and camp attendants. Meanwhile Friar Marcos de Niza added fuel to the fires of speculation about the stone city he had seen. Surely it had to be one of the seven fabled cities of gold. Soon, rumors were sweeping across Mexico City about women wearing beads of gold, and men dressed in fine white woolen robes. Silver was said to be available in incredible quantities. Indian blacksmiths made iron tools, and herdsmen had been seen tending cattle, sheep and pigs. A sense of hysterical urgency swept aside all reason. Although the Díaz party had only recently departed, Viceroy Mendoza found himself under increasing pressure to mount a full-scale expedition. There would be no problem finding citizens willing to invest their own gold and silver for supplies and men. Nor was there any difficulty finding volunteers who would risk the long journey to the Rio Grande Valley. Preparations were quickly underway. Mendoza selected a twenty-seven year old nobleman named Francisco Vásquez de Coronado, a former aide to the Viceroy, and territorial governor of one of the northern colonies. Coronado had proven himself an able soldier and honest administrator. Just as important, he was willing to risk his own substantial fortune helping to finance the expedition.

During the month of February, 1540, the young commander departed the town of Compostela some 450 miles northwest of Mexico City. He took with him 240 mounted soldiers, 60 more on foot, followed by 800 Indians, all armed, and hundreds more Indian camp attendants. The train included more than 1,000 pack animals, and a living commissary of several hundred head of sheep, cattle and pigs. Less than 200 miles into the journey Coronado met Melchior Díaz and his scouting party returning home. They were exhausted and near starvation. Several of Díaz' Indian porters had died from the winter cold. Worse, the explorer painted a dark picture of the country through which he had traveled. He had reached the southern New Mexico pueblos and found the people did possess limited amounts of cotton cloth and turquoise but no one had seen any evidence of gold or silver. Upon reaching the Zuñi village where Estéban had met his doom, the explorers were told the rapacious and dark-skinned mangod with the brass bells had been cut into pieces — carried into the desert and scattered. If he was indeed a god he would have been able to reassemble himself and return, but he had not. With that said the Díaz party was warned to turn back, and to instruct future intruders they would risk meeting the same fate. Melchior Díaz took the Indians' advice.

While the report by Díaz was sobering, there was no desire on the part of anyone in Coronado's expedition to retrace their own steps. For another 1,000 miles they trudged northward along the coastal regions of Mexico then northeast across southern Arizona. Friar de Niza rode with Coronado and his advance guard which soon ranged far ahead of the main column. Forage for their horses ran short. Animals collapsed and died. Food supplies ran low and morale began to decline, but Coronado pressed on.

Finally, on the morning of July 7, 1540, Coronado and 75 mounted soldiers and 25 more on foot, approached the Zuñi pueblo of Hawaikuh — the same town that had put an end to the sensuous appetites of the ill-fated Estéban. The Spaniards were met by armed Zuñis, and with interpreters, Coronado attempted to negotiate. His effort was met with a shower of arrows. The commander ordered a charge. In minutes a dozen Zuñis lay dead or dying. The remainder fled to the rooftops of the village, so closely pursued by soldiers that many had no time to pull up the ladders. Building stones were torn loose and hurled down on the attackers. Coronado was knocked off a ladder by a large stone and lay unconscious, but was quickly dragged to safety by several of his soldiers. In the end stones and arrows proved ineffective against matchlocks, shields, helmets, body armor and the sharp blades of halberds, swords and daggers.

Men, women and children fled their homes leaving everything to the invaders. Soldiers ransacked the houses, and in anger they cursed Friar Marcos de Niza to his face. There was no gold, no silver, and no precious jewels. The town was not what they had expected. Pedro de Castañeda, one of the expedition historians wrote that it was nothing more than

" . . . *a little crowded village, looking as if it had been crumpled all up together.*" Coronado penned a letter to Viceroy Mendoza then sent it south with a small party he instructed to return to the capital. Disgusted with Frey de Niza, and concerned the priest might be killed by angry expedition members, he sent the clergyman along. In the letter to the Viceroy he wrote that de Niza had " . . . *not told the truth in a single thing. The Seven Cities are seven little villages, all within a radius of thirteen miles.*" Nevertheless, Coronado made Hawaikuh his headquarters for the remainder of the winter.

As the rest of the expedition straggled in, other nearby towns were captured and occupied. Spanish officers ordered the inhabitants out and forced them to leave behind their winter food supplies. Coronado further demanded a large quantity of cotton cloth to be used as bedding for his men. He was told, honestly, that what he asked for did not exist.

Somewhere, the commander hoped, there were other cities more worthy of being conquered. Reconnaissance parties were sent out. One group of soldiers ranged far enough west to gaze into the depths of the Grand Canyon, a chasm so deep, they claimed, that no one would ever cross it. Another band of explorers traveled across the New Mexico mountains and onto the plains of northeastern New Mexico, as far as the Canadian River. There they saw, for the first time, great shaggy herds of bison beyond counting, dark rivers of living flesh stretching as far as the eye could see.

Winter passed slowly, especially for the exiled Zuñi people who had been forced to find shelter with neighboring tribes closer to the Rio Grande River. Fearing that their pueblos might be next, the residents began to show hostility towards Spanish patrols. To crush further opposition, Coronado took 200 men captive, had them tied to stakes and burned alive. Rather than break Indian resistance, the act only intensified it.

In desperation and rage the friends and families of the dead hurled themselves at the Spaniards, some with little more than stones and bare hands. Another 100 people died. Coronado, realizing he faced the possibility of a widespread revolt, decided to rip out the heart of Indian resistance.

In January of 1541, he attacked the town of Moho. Unable to break through the walls, the Spaniards began a siege hoping to take advantage of the fact the people had to bring their water in from the river. For two and a half months the town held out by surviving on melted snow water, and when that ran out, rather than surrender, the people of the pueblo threw themselves against Spanish steel. Women fought and died alongside their husbands. When the battle was over, more than 200 of the town's inhabitants had warmed the cold earth with their blood.

For the first time the Spaniards had suffered casualties too. That fact was not lost on the pueblo people, but sickened by the slaughter of previous months they wanted to end the bloodshed. They sent emissaries to ask for peace. Coronado's casualties at Moho had given the Spanish commander cause to rethink his own situation. It was agreed the Spaniards would do no more than erect crosses outside the towns and priests would give the people a rudimentary introduction to Christianity. The fighting ended.

Meanwhile stories of wealth resurfaced, this time from the mouth of a visiting Indian who had come from the northeast. His tribe was the Pawnee people, and he told about a land called Quivira, a land rich in gold, jewels, fine cloth and skilled artisans. During the third week of April, 1541, Coronado and most of his men left the Rio Grande Valley headed northeast towards Quivira. To guarantee the area inhabitants would remain peaceful while he was gone, he took a number of high-ranking captives with him.

For two months the column moved across the plains of Texas then north through Oklahoma. Coronado's men found only isolated villages consisting of small huts, naked children and barking dogs. There was no gold nor any other riches they could find. For another month the Spaniards lingered on the plains of Kansas, desperate to find something — anything. Coronado finally ordered the guide tortured. Had the Pawnee led the Spaniards into the grass country in hopes they might run out of supplies and die or was there another reason? The guide proved more resolute than his torturers. He said nothing. The embittered Coronado had him strangled. The seven cities of gold were either a myth or a lie.

Through the hot, drying days of August the expedition made its way southwest towards New Mexico where it spent a second winter. Supplies had been almost completely depleted, sickness struck, and men began deserting, heading back to Mexico in small groups, many never to be seen again. In the spring of 1542, the remnants of Coronado's once proud army marched south, reduced to a third of its original numbers. Deserters reached the capital well in advance of the main party. To protect themselves they denounced the expedition leader. When Coronado arrived in the capital he had already been branded a failure. He was given no opportunity to defend himself. He lived out the next twelve years of his life in obscurity — then died a ruined and broken man barely past his fortieth birthday.

When Coronado's men left the Rio Grande Valley that spring of 1542, several priests chose to remain behind. They were killed almost as soon as the Spaniards were out of sight. Forty years passed before the people of Zuñi and other New Mexico settlements saw more bearded men from the south. When they did return they came in handfuls, mostly men with families. Unlike the gold-hungry soldiers a half century earlier, these people were intent on living peacefully, farming, raising cattle and sheep, and trading with the pueblos. A few priests came with them. They were encouraged when they found the crosses Coronado's men had erected near Zuñi were still standing. The priests were allowed to build a mission, but few among the native people accepted the teachings of the Church, preferring instead to hold to ancestral beliefs.

War came again in 1680. Indian people up and down the Rio Grande Valley rose in revolt against the Spanish immigrants. The people of Zuñi did their part by killing their priest, but when the Rio Grande Valley was reoccupied twelve years later, authorities found the church at Zuñi still standing. The interior and furnishings had been carefully preserved by Indian believers and it was they who welcomed the new priest. In the decades that followed the Church co-existed with native ceremonies and Indian gods. It was in this world and among these people that Escalante ministered.

Nearly three weeks had passed since Domínguez and his followers had ridden into Zuñi. The horses and mules were rested and, having grazed freely in the nearby pastures, had put on flesh. The men were anxious to ride on, but before departing they participated in the Feast of Our Lady of Guadaloupe, in honor of the patron saint of the Zuñi Mission and of all Mexico. On the thirteenth day of December, 1776, the men swung into their saddles and began the final leg of their journey to Santa Fe.

"Because of various events we stayed in this mission until the 13th of December, when we left for La Villa de Santa Fe."

Dec. 13.

Chapter 10

LAST MILES
⊿ TO SANTA FE ⊾

The trail from Zuñi to Acoma was an ancient and well-marked eighty mile track heading due east through the desert country of western New Mexico. It was flanked on both sides by high sandstone bluffs and mesas. The first night the expedition camped on the southeast side of a cliff next to a large pool of water. The pool, permanently filled with rain or melt water funneling down from on top was deeper than the height of two men and more than a dozen yards across. Steps had been cut into the sandstone cliff behind the water to provide a way down from the top by a people who had vanished hundreds of years earlier. The step cutters left symbols and outlines of animals, pecked into the cliff face. On top of the mesa were the tumbled-in ruins of two small pueblos. The Zuñi people called them *"A'ts'ina."* The place of ghosts.

Generations of Spaniards had camped at the pool. Many had added their own names and messages to the rock *"On the 25th of the month of June, of this year of 1709, passed by here on the way to Zuñi — Ramon Garcia Jurado."* These visitors had named the place, El Morro, meaning "the headland." By Escalante's time, nearly two centuries of Spanish inscriptions reached from the east side around to the north — hundreds of yards of names and messages. The expedition left no

East of Zuñi on the way to El Morro Rock. This was an old established trail even in 1776. Escalante makes very little mention of the trip from this point to Santa Fe.

The expedition camped one night at El Morro National Monument east of Zuñi. Hundreds of Spanish inscriptions are engraved along the base of this giant cuesta but none have ever been found relating to Domínguez and Escalante.

inscriptions that cold and snowy December night. They were content to be sheltered from the wind, and secure beneath dry blankets. They missed the warmth of the quarters they had shared at Zuñi but their journey was almost over. They could easily bear a few more days of discomfort.

For the next two days the riders traversed a succession of low, rugged ridges where lava had once been squeezed from the depths of a tortured earth and then frozen into large, puddled mounds of black, wrinkled rock. Because of the snow, footing was treacherous and progress slow. Finally, the men were able to turn their horses towards the southeast and onto more open ground. Another day of travel put them in sight of two towering fortresses of stone soaring into a blue winter sky. A few puffy clouds lingered overhead, casting their shadows on the sandy earth, teasing the sun which had already banished much of the snow into the thirsty New Mexico earth. To the left was

Looking down from the top of El Morro at the campsite in the trees that the expedition would have used sometime during the second week of December. A deep permanent pool of water can be found next to the base of the rock.

Enchanted Mesa, a collection of closely-packed, uninhabited and almost unclimbable pinnacles of stone. Legends said they were once the home of the people of Acoma, and hidden within the crevices and gashes were shards of pottery and flakes of obsidian from a time no one could recall. The second mesa, a few arrow flights away, soared 400 feet upwards, and on its heights lived the people of Acoma.

When Spanish settlers began to enter the region, these were peaceful people who wished to be left alone but as the years passed they began to feel the increasingly harsh hand of the Spaniards. Eventually, tensions exploded. The nephew of the governor was killed at Acoma and the dead man's brother vowed revenge. Knowing his soldiers would never be able to fight their way up the narrow pathway that led to the village he waited until a January night in 1599. During hours of darkness Spanish soldiers quietly inched their way upwards through the fissures and gashes in the side of the mesa. By dawn they had gained the top, and were in position to attack the three terraces upon which the town had been built. A

" . . . we arrived at the mission of San Estéban de Acoma on the 16th day of the same December."

furious battle raged for three days, but Spanish steel and armor proved superior to wood and stone. The survivors of Acoma were forced to submit to the authority, and the religion, of their conquerors.

To commemorate their victory the Spaniards insisted the Acoma mission church be among the largest in the province, 150 feet long, 40 feet high and nearly as wide. Every stone and basket of adobe mud used in its construction was carried up from the desert floor below. Ceiling beams of pine more than 40 feet in length and a foot square were transported from the San Mateo Mountains twenty miles to the north, on the naked backs of sweating men, then inched up the narrow foot path to the top. It was impossible to dig graves in the grounds next to the church because the mesa top was solid stone. To provide a cemetery, a terrace wall of rock 45 feet high was built near the edge of the mesa top, then filled with earth carried up in baskets. Thirty years passed. A generation was gone and a new one had taken its place. The old ways and old memories were beginning to fade. Life was changing.

In 1629, in the name of the king of Spain, the church was presented with a painting of Saint Joseph. It was a grand painting and the citizens of Acoma prayed before it asking for the intercession of the father of Christ during drought and epidemics. Travelers asked for protection. Hunters too, requested favors. In time there were many accounts of how Joseph had blessed his Acoma children — with miracles. The people of Laguna, ten miles away, heard these stories. So it was, during a time of crisis, they asked if the people of their pueblo might borrow the painting. Their request was refused. Saint Joseph belonged to Acoma. His children made it known they were prepared to protect him just as fervently as he protected them.

All this was explained to Father Domínguez as he examined the church records and inspected the grounds. The walls of the church were nearly six feet thick. The site on which it had been built slanted making it necessary to build a level floor with adobe mud a few inches thick on one end and a foot and a half thick on the other. For that reason there were no burials within the church walls. The interior was plain but pleasant.

The parish books were neatly done and nearly full. He ordered three new ones, and left orders when they arrived the old ones were to be sent to Santa Fe to be placed in the archives. Outside the church were several small trees and shrubs. Domínguez was told that to keep them alive in their shallow beds of transported earth it was necessary, during the

Most of the missions that Domínguez inspected have changed considerably in the past two centuries. One notable exception is the San Miguel Mission in Santa Fe which was built shortly after the town was established in 1609. It is well preserved and open to the public.

growing season, for twelve women to each bring a daily jar of water from the bottom of the mesa to pour into the dry earth. Each watering was a living prayer, a gift to God. It was an object lesson that pleased the inspector. As the plants were nourished by the devotion of the women so were the lives of the Acoma people nourished by the love of God.

The town had recently been experiencing hard times. Four years of drought had reduced the population from 1,114 people to 530. The pueblo had no access to irrigation and depended entirely on rainfall. Hope was returning in the fact there had been more rain that previous summer and the recent snows were giving promise the worst was over. Another heavy snow fell the night of December 16. Saint Joseph had not forgotten his children.

Four days later clearing skies and warming temperatures allowed the expedition to press on towards Laguna, a half day's ride to the northeast. Unlike Acoma with its one defensible pathway, Laguna was built on the top of an easily-accessible hill. It was a relatively new town, having been founded by a Franciscan priest named Antonio Miranda, who, in the words of Fray Juan Sanz de Lezaun, " . . . *went throughout all the land, even to the most rugged sierras, collecting the wandering sheep of numerous nations."*

On July 4, 1699, Miranda and his band of Indian followers founded the village of San José de la Laguna. The soil was rich and crops flourished. People even moved to Laguna from Acoma. Together they built their own mission church. It was not as large as the one at Acoma but different in that it was constructed of stone and had apartments, guest quarters, and administrative offices connected to one side. The interior was richly decorated with brightly painted walls, squared ceiling timbers, portraits of saints, and a rich variety of Christian symbols. Intermixed were representations of the sun, moon, stars and a rainbow — a marriage of carvings intertwining Indian and Catholic imagery. The windows in the mission as well as the nearby homes were covered with semi-transparent sheets of crystallized gypsum. The expedition remained in Laguna for one day, enough time for Father Domínguez to complete his inspection of the mission records. He recorded two brass candlesticks, two small brass bells and a crucifix. On the wall behind the altar hung a crude painting of Saint Joseph done on a piece of buffalo hide. When the people of Acoma had refused to lend Laguna their painting of the saint, it had been decided to paint one of their own. Domínguez noted in his report that the parish registers were full. He left several sheets of paper and ordered new books. As to how the mission priest survived he had this to say, " . . . *the father is given a sheep a week, and . . . beans, eggs, lard, salt, flour, a tallow candle and milk in the summer every day.*" These items were collected by the native parishioners on a rotating basis. Everyone was involved. Of the peoples' houses Domínguez wrote, " . . . *the interiors are always very clean and all the exterior walls are white-washed so that the pueblo can be seen from afar on any road because it is so white.*"

The expedition journeyed on to Isleta, a two day ride east by southeast. The name means *"little island,"* which reflected the location of the town, between an arroyo and the Rio Grande River. It was the largest of the river settlements, and had always been friendly towards the Spaniards. The rich river bottom lands allowed the settlement to grow rapidly. By 1629, it had completed a beautiful church, and in 1680, Isleta counted nearly 2,000 inhabitants. When word reached the pueblo of the revolt in Santa Fe, nearly the entire population fled south to El Paso with the Spaniards. Other Indians came, looted the town and burned the church. The walls and mission compound were used as corrals. When the region was re-conquered a decade later the church at Isleta was rebuilt, bigger and more beautiful than before. Walls were 110 feet long and nearly 30 feet wide. Not content with one saint, paintings of Saint Bartholomew, Our Lady of Guadaloupe and other holy people adorned the walls. Carved figures of Mary and Joseph stood behind the altar. Beneath the earth floor rested the bones of one of the early priests — no one could tell Domínguez exactly who.

Neither could the resident priest explain why he personally owned forty bushels of wheat and corn as well as ten sheep, six strings of chilies, a container of lard, two wax candles and other items Domínguez felt were beyond the needs of a parish priest. The inspector sternly reminded the offending cleric about the meaning of the three knots in the rope sash he wore around his waist — poverty, chastity and charity. The Isleta priest was ordered to re-examine his vow of poverty and make a complete confession, in writing, to his provincial superior.

It was in Isleta the expedition celebrated Christmas Eve. When darkness came, dozens and then hundreds of small fires flickered from nearby hillsides surrounding the pueblo. Each one had been lit to symbolize the light and warmth brought into the world by the Christ child almost eighteen centuries earlier. After the celebration it was north to Santa Fe.

"We left El Pueblo de la Isleta, and after going 13 miles we arrived at the mission of San Francisco Xavier de Albuquerque."

Dec. 28.

In quick succession the riders passed through the mission settlements of Albuquerque, Sandia and Santo Domingo. The first day of the new year was spent in the saddle — the Capital was only hours away. Even the horses and mules had picked up their step, seemingly aware they were near the end of their own journey.

"On the 2nd of January of this year of '77 we reached La Villa de Santa Fe." The Santa Fe Plaza today where the expedition began and ended.

Two days later Escalante penned, in the final journal entry, *"On the 3rd of January we presented this diary, the painted token of the Lagunas which received mention therein, and the Laguna Indian. And because everything contained in this diary is true and faithful to what occurred and was observed during our journey, we do sign it on this same 3rd day of January of the year 1777."* Fray Francisco Atanasio Domínguez, and his subordinate, Fray Silvestre Vélez de Escalante, attached their signatures and presented the journal to the governor. Father Domínguez made apologies for having taken longer than first communicated in his letter from Zuñi. The snow storms and the condition of their horses made them delay longer than they intended. In addition, he had chosen to complete his inspection of missions, and that had added to their travel time.

Their journey had taken 159 days and covered over 1,700 miles. Although it had not reached California, the expedition traveled across and explored regions that had previously been unknown to the Spanish. No one had fired a shot in anger or defense, and none of the expedition members suffered serious injury or death. The governor was presented with the painted deer skin the padres had obtained from the Laguna people at Utah Lake the previous September, and was introduced to the Laguna boy, Joachín. Domínguez praised the services the lad provided as a translator, and announced he would be returning with the priests during the summer of 1777, when they returned to Utah Lake.

The governor listened, but made few comments. He seemed preoccupied or unfriendly, Domínguez could not determine which. Neither did he warm to Joachín beyond the briefest of acknowledgments. The priests finally excused themselves, and they and the boy left for their quarters. Captain Miera remained behind to see that the men were paid according to agreements made the previous July. The remaining trade goods were inventoried and placed in safe keeping. The animals were taken away. The journey had ended.

Chapter 11

⊿ EPILOGUE ⊾

S everal days passed. Domínguez understood the mood of his
secular superior the morning he had been presented with
the journal. The governor and his inner circle of friends were
genuinely upset the expedition had not reached Monterey.
Their investment in the trip had yielded nothing. Governor
Mendinueta feared the failure to reach California would reflect
on his own situation. He had enough to worry about with the
continuing attacks by Comanche and Apache raiders. Then
there was the festering matter of Father Domínguez. The priest
from Mexico City had ignited a firestorm the previous summer
and the governor and his friends were involved.

The head of the New Mexico missions had spared nothing in his report. His accounts of priests participating in moral
improprieties and involving themselves in other worldly
activities had deeply disturbed the Franciscan superiors in
Mexico City. Government officials had also read the letters.
For decades both church and state had assumed all was well on
the northern frontier. Neither had Domínguez kept back
details about crumbling and poverty stricken missions that, in
their attempts to survive, had transferred tracts of church land
to secular owners—some of whom were more than casual
acquaintances of the governor.

Governor Mendinueta was not the only one concerned about the report. There were the offending priests who had much to lose, a handful of men determined they would not go down without a fight. They were individuals who had powerful family connections in Mexico City and the royal court of Spain. Father Domínguez might be head of the New Mexico missions, but he was an unknown provincial with little backing beyond that of his ecclesiastical superiors.

Once it was certain his report had been posted south to the Capital, the conspirators went into action. They followed Domínguez' communications with their own. They accused the inspector of accepting bribes from members of the clergy to whom he had given high marks. Domínguez' superiors might have dismissed one or two letters — but there were enough to raise questions about the head of missions, however honest he had proven to be in the past.

When Father Domínguez learned of the charges against him he immediately set out for Mexico City to mount a defense. His journey ended a short ways south of El Paso. He was intercepted by a letter that relieved him of all administrative duties. He was to remain in El Paso and subsequently be reassigned as a parish priest in one of the outlying presidios of northern Mexico. He had been placed in exile.

For a time the former inspector fought back. In one letter dated August 16, 1777, he wrote, " . . . *I have not even accepted chocolate, and have made them all take some of what I had with me; that I have favored the friars sometimes with cigars, sometimes with chocolate, sometimes giving them all they asked me for? Does not this suffice, I say, to remove even the slightest suspicion there may possibly be against my good conduct?*" Despite his efforts, this and other letters remained unanswered.

An attempt was made to make the former expedition leader pay for the horses his men had eaten during their trek across Arizona. That effort failed. Domínguez, true to his vows of poverty, had nothing with which to pay. The five month journal he and Escalante had collaborated on was filed away and never seen again. Had it not been for a second copy made while the original was yet in Santa Fe, the contents might have been lost forever. As to the reports Domínguez had sent to his superiors, these too were filed away and forgotten — one with the notation, *"This report is intended to be a description of New Mexico, but its phraseology is obscure, it lacks proportion, and offers little to the discriminating taste."* The documents, rediscovered and published in 1956, are today considered some of the most significant and detailed accounts about life in the early New Mexico region.

Domínguez never really accepted the decision of his superiors. As late as May 1, 1795, he was still trying to defend himself. In a letter, of that date, to his provincial supervisor he wrote, *" . . . there are in my possession documents to prove my claims in and out of court."* His only response was continued silence. Father Domínguez remained in the northern territories for the remainder of his life, serving at one mission outpost and then another. He died in late winter of 1805, at the age of sixty-five, in Sonora, Mexico, a forgotten man.

Almost immediately after the expedition had ended Father Silvestre Vélez De Escalante was transferred from the mission at Zuñi to a newer work at San Ildefonso, a short distance northwest of Santa Fe. Even before Escalante had been selected to accompany the expedition to Monterey, his descriptive and analytical reports had come to the attention of his ecclesiastical superiors as well as government officials. As a missionary priest he continued to travel throughout the New Mexico region, writing reports and gathering historical material. By the winter of 1780, Escalante had completed a summary of New Mexico history from 1693 to 1715. Then, the excruciating pain that had almost kept him from joining the 1776 expedition returned. This time there was no relief.

He asked permission to journey to Mexico City in search of medical treatment but died on the trail near Parral, Mexico, in April 1780, from what is believed to be kidney failure. He was thirty years old. Escalante's was not the only death that spring. Smallpox came north on the same trail and struck New Mexico. By the autumn of 1781, more than 5,000 New Mexico Indians had perished along with many Spanish settlers. Several missions were so depopulated they had to be abandoned.

Captain Don Bernardo Miera Y Pacheco, the expedition cartographer, busied himself after returning to Santa Fe tending to his own private affairs and his ranching activities. During that time he drew a map of the regions the expedition had passed through, an elaborate work complete with drawings and illustrations. Slightly below the Great Salt Lake, and on the left margin of the map he left a blank space and wrote the words, *"the unknown land."* The captain was a talented artist. Those who viewed the map found themselves drawn to that blank spot. What lay beyond? Miera was never completely convinced the expedition should have turned south at Utah Lake. California, he believed, could not have been more than a week or so of travel further west. Although he never had the opportunity to return and test his theory, his map was reproduced, and stories of the great salty inland sea he had included reached the ears of American trapping brigades a generation later and it was a handful of American beaver trappers who made the first trek across Miera's blank spot. As it turned out it was not a trip of one week but of many and across deserts and mountains that killed both men and animals. There is no doubt if the Domínguez' expedition had attempted this route during the winter, they would have perished.

In addition to a copy of his map, Captain Miera wrote a lengthy letter to the king of Spain dated October 26, 1777. In it he gave an abbreviated account of the journey. He also laid out a plan to establish three new Spanish colonies, the largest of which would be in the valley south of the Great Salt Lake. Miera spelled out, in great detail, the potential of the region, *"It alone is capable of maintaining a settlement with as many people as Mexico City . . . ."* Miera also made an impassioned plea for expanding mission activity into the new lands. *"But in order to succeed in bringing about the salvation of these souls, some difficulties will have to be overcome, namely the great distance, and the obstacle imposed by [enemies] . . . which at present ravages these provinces."*

Captain Miera presented a plan to reform colonial troops to include fast moving, lightly armed companies of cavalry and mounted infantry. Near the end of his letter, Miera suggested the future of Spain's holdings in the American southwest depended on a rapid influx of Spanish settlers, new missions and a stronger military presence. Although admitting a venture of this size would initially be expensive, he expressed the opinion the region held vast reserves of gold and silver — far in excess of the costs incurred by the government. Miera's map and report were well received in the Spanish court but no action was taken. The king and his ministers were concerned with a more immediate problem in the northern colonies.

For nearly two years, Governor Mendinueta had made unsuccessful attempts to deal with increasingly violent raids by Comanche warriors on Spanish settlements and nearby Indian pueblos. His lack of success, and perhaps some of the revelations by Father Domínguez, led to his political downfall. He was replaced by Don Juan Bautista de Anza, who had come to the notice of King Carlos III after having opened the first successful trail into California in 1775. The new governor arrived in Santa Fe to find only 80 soldiers and their officers. He met Miera and read a copy of the captain's report to King Carlos. He was particularly drawn to Miera's ideas about fast moving and lightly armed cavalry. Traditional Spanish tactics called for ground forces followed by clumsy carts filled with supplies. An army on the move produced a cloud of dust that betrayed its position days in advance. There was no way it could force engagement with mounted Indian warriors. Cavalry had traditionally been used for scouting — not fighting. Miera convinced the new governor that mounted troops, traveling with a minimum of supplies, during the hours of darkness, would prove successful. The idea was approved and put into operation.

Governor de Anza's first target was a band of Comanches that wintered along the front range mountains of Colorado south of present day Colorado Springs. These were the Yamparika Comanche, the same people who, it is believed, had given the Domínguez-Escalante party concern when they passed through northwestern Colorado the previous autumn. They took their name from the Yampa River of northwestern Colorado, their home before they migrated out of the mountains and onto the plains to raid Spanish settlements and New Mexico ranches.

The Yamparikas had grown more bold and their raids had been penetrating deeper into New Mexico. Their leader, a chief called Green Horn, made no secret of his contempt for traditional Spanish tactics. He knew slow moving infantry would never get close enough to attack his mounted warriors.

Governor de Anza intended to change that. He took his 80 regulars and 200 newly trained and mounted militia members, followed by 300 mounted Ute Indian allies, through the San Luis Valley and north into South Park. Even though the mountains were between his troops and the Comanche, de Anza's men rode at night to avoid any tell-tale dust plume and made no fires — a hardship because the men were unable to cook. West of Colorado Springs the column turned east, out of the mountains onto the plains, north of, and behind, Green Horn's people.

Many Comanche warriors did not have time to catch their horses before the Spanish were upon them. They could stand and fight or run. For several miles they left a trail of dead. More than 500 horses were rounded up along with several dozen women and children. It was they who told de Anza that Green Horn and many of his warriors were expected home any day from yet another raid on the New Mexico settlements. The governor and his troops picked their ground and waited. Two days later, in late afternoon, Green Horn and his unsuspecting warriors rode into the trap. Spanish steel soon had the Comanches in retreat. Pursuit continued under a bright moon. Governor de Anza had no intention of allowing the escape of the chief with the headdress of green painted buffalo horns. By first light the exhausted Comanche warriors were surrounded. When it was over Green Horn lay dead. Also killed was his eldest son, four minor chiefs and a medicine man who claimed to be immortal. The Yamparika Comanche threat ended. Captain Miera's methods of warfare had proven effective. There would be other battles for the graying old captain, all victorious. He was able to watch his sons, Cleto and Manuel, rise to prominence in New Mexico affairs. Miera died of natural causes in 1785.

Despite the efforts of various researchers the remaining members of the Expedition of 1776-77, faded into the obscurity from which they had come. To their frontier contemporaries, a 1,700 mile journey through the wilderness of the southwest had not been particularly noteworthy. It is only through the survival of a copy of the expedition journal that some of their names are remembered at all. Still, through those daily entries, so meticulously kept by Escalante, and in some cases Domínguez, the reader is allowed to glimpse fragments of personalities representative of the early Spanish frontier.

Don Pedro Cisneros and Don Joaquín Laín, perhaps more than the others, represented the restless impatience of many Spaniards of that day. These were men who, even though they had wealth to live comfortable and safe lives, exhibited a continuing sense of curiosity and adventure. They were willing to take risks. Cisneros does not show up in any records after 1776. The only other reference researchers have found concerning this former official of the Zuñi pueblo is a land sale his family made in 1754. References to Laín have turned up three times, two marriages and finally his death in 1799.

Lorenzo Oliveres and Juan De Aguilar, known almost entirely by the brief notations by their names in the beginning of the journal were the caliber of men who knew how to take a string of pack animals through almost any kind of terrain. Aguilar's name also appears in the records. He married Isabel Gutiérrez in Bernalillo, New Mexico, September 24, 1781.

Andrés Muñíz the expedition interpreter, a Hispanicized Indian trader, caused Domínguez and Escalante considerable trouble and exasperation during the journey. He was a man who chose to listen to his own instincts before he submitted to authority. His brother, Antonio Lucrecio, was skilled enough in frontier living to swim the Colorado River in November naked, on horseback, and then make his way back to the expedition three grueling days later — all with no ill effects.

The two runaways, Juan Domingo and Felipe, who joined with the expedition in southwestern Colorado proved able and willing scouts, not adverse to putting their lives at risk in the expedition's quest to cross the gorge of the Grand

Canyon. Escalante recorded their efforts during this phase of the expedition and does not mention them again.

It is probable that Simón Lucero, servant to Don Pedro Cisneros was not out of his teens but when his master pushed him too far during those tense days south of Utah Lake, he did not hesitate to take the older individual to the ground. He was a man first and a servant second — a typical example of frontier thinking.

There was the first Ute Indian they had met and named Atanasio. Escalante noted the man turned over the two hunting knives and sixteen strands of glass beads to his wife, not even keeping one of the knives for himself, before he left his family to lead the expedition north along the Uncompahgre Plateau towards Grand Mesa. Atanasio was taking a risk. He did not know these people he had agreed to guide. Perhaps they would kill him when his usefulness was at an end. He made certain they could not take back the valuable trade items he had bartered for.

Silvestre, the Laguna Ute who agreed to guide the expedition from Grand Mesa into Utah, could not have failed to understand that, at times, he rode under a cloud of simmering suspicion. He continued on and fulfilled his commitment with no complaint. Without his intimate knowledge about the lands of northwestern Colorado and northeastern Utah, and his ability to find water, it is doubtful the expedition would have reached Utah Lake.

Joaquín also vanished. Escalante never explained how the young Laguna came to be with the Utes on Grand Mesa. The fact he joined the expedition seems to be an impetuous act. That September morning as the men were riding away from the Ute camp he suddenly burst onto the scene wanting to return to Utah Lake and home. There was no time to bridle a horse for him. Don Joaquín Laín simply reached down and pulled the boy up behind and continued on. It was from Laín that Joaquín took his name. Escalante made no attempt to record what the boy was called in his own tongue. It is obvious he found his way into the hearts of the expedition members because two weeks later he was on the back of one of the best horses — racing the animal across a grassy flat when it fell and was mortally injured. In Escalante's words the unhurt Joaquín *"was shedding a flood of tears."* He feared not only the injuries of the horse but that he had angered his new friends.

Neither is it told why Joaquín insisted on continuing with the expedition when it departed the Laguna camps at Utah Lake. He might have been an orphan because nothing is said about him having a family. Either way it is obvious he developed a great attachment to Escalante and Domínguez, sleeping between them and caring for their horses. After the new Laguna guide, José María, abandoned the expedition two weeks south of Utah Lake, Joaquín's presence took on new meaning. The various bands of Paiute people the Spaniards encountered were more willing to have contact with a party traveling with a boy, and Joaquín was able to serve as interpreter when Andrés could no longer understand the changing dialects they began to encounter. Never once is there any indication in the journal that the lad complained or failed in what he perceived as his responsibilities and duties. He is mentioned often as an interpreter, a contact person to the Paiutes or as a scout — all duties of a grown man.

Nothing is known about Joaquín's life after the expedition was disbanded. What is probable is that he remained in the Santa Fe area, and under the watchful eyes of Escalante, integrated himself into a new life. Many Indians did exactly that and often quite successfully. It is just as possible the boy may have returned to Utah Lake at some point later on.

The explorer/priest Fray Francisco Garcés must not be forgotten. His letter to Escalante had prevented the expedition from attempting to reach California by going straight across Arizona. He had warned about the great canyon, dry deserts and hostile tribes and it was a warning the expedition heeded. During the summer of 1781, Father Garcés was attacked and clubbed to death outside his church in southwestern Arizona by Yuma Indians.

It was an uprising not unlike the one that had temporarily driven the Spanish out of the Rio Grande Valley in 1680. Although on a much smaller scale, the Yuma people and their allies did force the Spanish settlers out of the Lower Colorado basin after killing more than fifty men and capturing seventy women and children, who were kept as slaves. The road that de Anza and Garcés had opened a few years earlier was subsequently abandoned. With this land route to California closed, the coastal settlements began to become self-contained. Contact with Mexico City became more sporadic. With rich soils and mild climate the descendants of the original coastal settlers prospered.

A trail did open some years later from Santa Fe to California and it carried traders who packed New Mexico wool blankets to the coast and traded them for horses and mules. In the 1840s, a number of families from the Rio Grande Valley migrated to California over the trail, carrying all their belongings on pack mules. This torturous track followed only part of the route traveled by Domínguez and Escalante and was laid out to take advantage of available water and forage — a significant problem especially during dry years. It was a lack of these two necessities as well as difficult terrain that led the Expedition of 1776 so far north into Colorado before it turned west.

Spain never did attempt to act on Captain Miera's advice to develop the colonies he proposed. Vastly rich with colonial gold and silver, the Spanish Crown was caught up in affairs closer to her own borders. European wars were beginning to bleed away the nation's wealth and power.

In 1808, this once proud empire fell under the control of France. New masters sailed west across the Atlantic, but Mexico refused to recognize the government set in place by Napoleon. Mexican nationals rose up to throw off the French yoke. For more than a decade this old Spanish colony was rocked by battles and uprisings.

By 1821, Mexico was an independent nation, although financially destitute and struggling for survival. Again the northern colonies were ignored. California was too far away to govern effectively, and with its small population of ranchers and agriculturists, produced little in the way of potential revenues beyond cattle hides that were picked up by occasional visiting ships. To complicate matters further, the Californians displayed resistance to interference by Mexico City — especially tax collectors.

It was not much different in the Rio Grande Valley. It took nearly three years for supply trains to make the trip from the Capital north to Santa Fe and back again, a total distance of nearly 4,000 miles. Spain had forbidden commerce with the new United States but after independence had been declared, Mexico lifted the ban. In a short time wagon trains rumbled westward along the newly opened Santa Fe Trail which stretched from Missouri, across Kansas and into southeastern Colorado before turning south into New Mexico over Raton Pass. It was an easy trail of a little over 700 miles and there were many in New Mexico who were eager to exchange Mexican silver for American manufactured goods.

American settlers began moving into Texas, and within a few years, wrenched it from Mexican control. It was a victory that soon had Washington politicians speaking loudly about the divine right of Americans to move westward and occupy the new lands they traveled through. War followed and New Mexico fell to the United States in 1846, with California also falling under American control — with all the lands in between. In the months and years that followed American immigrants poured into the southwest in ever-increasing numbers. Few had any regard for the rights of former Mexican colonials or the Indians.

In retrospect, Captain Miera's 1777 letter to the king of Spain was prophetic. The potential settlement he spoke of near Utah Lake was established, not by Spaniards but by Mormon settlers less than a half century later and today the region is one of the showplaces of America. His ideas about combating hostile Indians, so successfully initiated by Governor de Anza, were used by the American army to subdue other native peoples of the west. His speculation that exploration and settlement costs to the Crown would eventually be regained through the return of gold and silver also proved true. The United States took incredible quantities of these and other minerals out of California, Nevada and Colorado.

Escalante has been proven correct in the potential he saw for building towns and agricultural enterprises in the places through which the expedition passed. On August 26, 1776, he paused on a small rise in the Uncompahgre Valley, south of the city of Montrose, Colorado, and penned these words, *"Here it has . . . good land for farming with the help of irrigation . . . . There is all the rest needed for establishing a good settlement . . . ."* A hundred years later the valley was on its way to becoming an agricultural paradise — with the help of irrigation.

For the final five months of 1776, two Franciscan priests, a retired army captain, two native Spaniards, a few Mixed Bloods, Indians and one impetuous boy rode across 1,700 miles of wilderness, exploring, preaching and reaching out to those they met. Not a shot was fired in anger or defense, and there was no loss of human life. Material costs were limited to a few unfortunate horses, an insignificant quantity of supplies, wages and little more than one hundred pounds of trade goods. Had Domínguez been allowed to return to Utah Lake the following summer as he had proposed, he would have gone on to Monterey. Captain Miera intended to map the Great Salt Lake and explore points beyond. A different chapter to Spanish colonial history could have been written. The American West might be different today had these men been allowed to continue on. It was not to be. The letters of corrupt priests, warring Comanche raiders, Napoleon, a weakening Spanish interest in the new world, Manifest Destiny, and an American war with Mexico — all were waiting to write their own words across the pages of history.

Endnotes

CHAPTER 1. The quotes and much of the background information for this chapter have been taken from Adam's and Chavez' book *The Missions of New Mexico, 1776: A Description by Fray Francisco Atanasio Domínguez With Other Contemporary Documents.*

CHAPTER 3. It has been a point of controversy with various scholars as to whether the Indians referred to by the Grand Mesa Utes really were Comanche or members of some other tribe. Andrew Isenberg, on page 34 of his book, *The Destruction of the Bison*, makes a very strong argument that these were actually Comanches.

CHAPTERS 3 THROUGH 8. All quotes in these chapters have been taken directly from Warner and Chavez' translation of *The Dominguez Escalante Journal: Their Expedition Through Colorado, Utah, Arizona, and New Mexico in 1776.* The exceptions are where, for ease of understanding, I have changed Fray Chavez' use of Spanish leagues into English miles.

CHAPTER 9. Much of the historical information contained in this chapter comes from Adams and Chavez' book, *The Missions of New Mexico* referred to in Chapter 1.

CHAPTER 10. The inscription on the rock and other information pertaining to the campsite at El Morro have been taken from the Western National Parks Association publication, *El Morro Trails: El Morro National Monument.* Details about the missions in this chapter come from documents contained in Adams and Chavez' book, *The Missions of New Mexico.*

CHAPTER 11. *The Missions of New Mexico* continues to provide material for this chapter. Details about the Comanche campaign of 1779 were taken from George Hyde's book, Indians of the High Plains and Ronald Kessler's work, *Anza's 1779 Comanche Campaign*.

Bibliography

Adams, Eleanor B. And Fray Chavez, Angelico. *The Missions of New Mexico, 1776: A Description by Fray Francisco Atanasio Domínguez With Other Contemporary Documents*. Albuquerque, NM: The University of New Mexico Press. 1956.

Bannon, John Francis. *Bolton and the Spanish Borderlands*. Norman, OK: University of Oklahoma Press. 1964.

Barker, Ruth Laughlin. *Caballeros*. New York, NY: D. Appleton & Company. 1931.

Bolton, Herbert E. *Pageant In the Wilderness*. Salt Lake City, UT: Utah State Historical Society. 1950.

Cerquone, Joseph. *In Behalf of the Light: The Domínguez and Escalante Expedition of 1776*. Denver, CO: Bicentennial Expedition, Inc. 1976.

Hyde, George E. *Indians of the High Plains*. Norman, OK: University of Oklahoma Press. 1959.

Isenberg, Andrew C. *The Destruction of the Bison*. Cambridge, UK: Cambridge University Press. 2000.

Kessler, Ronald E. *Anza's 1779 Comanche Campaign*. Monte Vista, CO: Ronald E. Kessler. 1994.

Prince, L. Bradford. *Spanish Mission Churches of New Mexico*. Glorieta, NM: The Rio Grande Press, Inc. 1977.

Vandenbusche, Duane and Smith, Duane A. *A Land Alone: Colorado's Western Slope*. Boulder, CO: Pruett Publishing Company. 1981.

Warner, Ted J. (Editor) and Chavez, Fray Angelico. (Translator) *The Domínguez Escalante Journal: Their Expedition through Colorado, Utah, Arizona, and New Mexico in 1776*. Salt Lake City, UT: University of Utah Press. 1995.

Miscellaneous Material:

El Morro Trails: El Morro National Monument, New Mexico. Western National Parks Association.

Miller, David E. (Editor) *The Route of the Domínguez — Escalante Expedition 1776-77. A Report of Trail Research Conducted Under the Auspices of the Domínguez — Escalante State/Federal Bicentennial Committee and the Four Corners Regional Commission*. 1976.

Ken Reyher has always had an interest in how people of earlier times lived on a day-to-day basis. His formal introduction to the subject came during training he received while he was an airman during the Viet Nam War. He learned that methods of living and surviving under primitive conditions have changed little over thousands of years.

After his military service Reyher taught high school history and frequently included his knowledge about the era of the fur trappers and Plains Indians. His students learned to make fire with flint and steel, and practiced other skills now largely forgotten. On one occasion his American History class turned a wet, bloody buffalo hide into a brain-tanned robe, the Indian way, on the floor of his classroom.

After retiring from teaching Reyher began taking solo trips along old western trails, on foot or by horseback. He is well acquainted with the clothing, tools, technology and foods that were available two centuries ago. His knowledge and experience have grown as have the miles that he has covered. His most recent project has been the Domínguez — Escalante Trail, a 1,700 mile loop that began in Santa Fe, New Mexico, wound its way up through western Colorado (passing two miles from Reyher's home) then through Utah, across northern Arizona and back to Santa Fe. Over a two year period, Reyher followed or paralleled the entire route, be it on foot, by horse, riding his motorcycle or in his pickup. Almost half his journey he was accompanied by his son, Marc, who, with an advanced GPS unit, proved to be a very competent navigator. (Always close at hand was a dog-eared copy of the journal that had been kept by the 1776 expedition.) Reyher made extensive use of the field notes compiled by teams of researchers who had located most of the significant points along the route in the months prior to the 1976 bi-centennial of the expedition.